SpringerBriefs in Psychology

SpringerBriefs present concise summaries of cutting-edge research and practical applications across a wide spectrum of fields. Featuring compact volumes of 50 to 125 pages, the series covers a range of content from professional to academic. Typical topics might include:

- A timely report of state-of-the-art analytical techniques
- A bridge between new research results as published in journal articles and a contextual literature review
- A snapshot of a hot or emerging topic
- An in-depth case study or clinical example
- A presentation of core concepts that readers must understand to make independent contributions

SpringerBriefs in Psychology showcase emerging theory, empirical research, and practical application in a wide variety of topics in psychology and related fields. Briefs are characterized by fast, global electronic dissemination, standard publishing contracts, standardized manuscript preparation and formatting guidelines, and expedited production schedules.

More information about this series at http://www.springer.com/series/10143

Cameron McIntosh • Katy O'Neill

Evidence-Based Treatments for Problem Gambling

Springer

Cameron McIntosh
St Vincent's Hospital Gambling Treatment Program
St Vincent's Hospital
Sydney, NSW, Australia

Katy O'Neill
St Vincent's Hospital Gambling Treatment Program
St Vincent's Hospital
Sydney, NSW, Australia

ISSN 2192-8363 ISSN 2192-8371 (electronic)
SpringerBriefs in Psychology
ISBN 978-3-319-62484-6 ISBN 978-3-319-62485-3 (eBook)
DOI 10.1007/978-3-319-62485-3

Library of Congress Control Number: 2017947874

Printed on acid-free paper

This Springer imprint is published by Springer Nature
The registered company is Springer International Publishing AG
The registered company address is: Gewerbestrasse 11, 6330 Cham, Switzerland

Preface

Problem gambling treatments continue to develop; however, the literature in this area is not as vast as that for other addictions, most notably substance and alcohol misuse treatments. As cognitive behavior therapy (CBT) has been refined, and so called third-wave therapies have been developed to focus upon psychopathology over the last few decades, we have seen opportunities to apply some of these "newer" techniques to problem gamblers in our clinic. We believe that such a process has merit due to the success many of these approaches have reported with disorders that commonly appear comorbidly with problem gambling. Over this time, we have observed some healthy debate among clinicians about the contribution that some of the newer therapies bring to treatment beyond CBT. As is common in other treatment areas, CBT maintains the greatest levels of empirical support for problem gambling treatment and has provided a valid framework to assist many problem gamblers recover.

We believe that it is critical for our clients that the literature be developed by exploring new treatments in evidence-based ways. It is also very clear that the strategies of one therapy can easily overlap with the strategies of another, given the shared theoretical basis and common goal to improve treatment outcomes. There appears to be many ways to explain the same phenomenon, and given the diverse nature of individuals affected by problem gambling, there is also likely to be diversity in the way treatment is experienced by an individual. There are clearly many variables across successful treatment. Case conceptualization provides an example of this point, as very little research supports the inclusion of case conceptualizations due to the confounding effect they can have on protocols, yet most effective clinicians would not work without one. Although there is "room" in the treatment of this population for some eclectic treatments given the current status of the literature, we believe that it is incumbent on clinicians to use treatments in accordance with the existing literature or with an appropriate research focus.

In writing this book, we have attempted to provide the evidence base for the major contemporary treatments that can be applied to problem gambling. Many approaches described within have only an introductory level of research supporting them for this population, while others despite an extensive literature are still open to development. Our aims in compiling the chapters that make up this book were to help clinicians find their "therapeutic voice," promote further clinical research for problem gamblers to develop the literature, and most importantly to try and contribute to the overall treatment effectiveness of this often debilitating disorder.

Sydney, NSW, Australia

Cameron McIntosh
Katy O'Neill

Abbreviations

AVE	Abstinence Violation Effect
ACT	Acceptance and Commitment Therapy
APA	American Psychiatric Association
BPD	Borderline Personality Disorder
CBT	Cognitive Behavioral Therapy
DBT	Dialectical Behavior Therapy
DSM	Diagnostic and Statistical Manual
EGM	Electronic Gaming Machine
EI	Elaborated Intrusion
EMS	Early Maladaptive Schema(s)
fMRI	Functional Magnetic Resonance Imaging
GABA	Gamma-Aminobutyric Acid
GRCS	Gambling-Related Cognitions Scale
MBCT	Mindfulness-Based Cognitive Therapy
MBRP	Mindfulness-Based Relapse Prevention
MI	Motivational Interviewing
NAC	N-Acetylcysteine
NTX	Naltrexone
PG	Problem Gambling or Problem Gambler
PGRTC	Problem Gambling Research and Treatment Centre
PGSI	Problem Gambling Severity Index
RP	Relapse Prevention
RNG	Random Number Generator
SMA	Schema Mode Approach
SSRI	Selective Serotonin Reuptake Inhibitor
SUDs	Substance Use Disorders
TAU	Treatment as Usual
TOD	Time on Device
YSQ	Young Schema Questionnaire

Contents

About the Authors

Cameron McIntosh, BComm, MLLR, MBA, Grad Dip Psych, BSc (Hons), MPsych (Clinical), DPsych is a Sydney, Australia-based clinical psychologist. He worked at the St Vincent's Hospital Gambling Treatment Program where he became the team leader and in private practice for the 5 years prior to this publication. Cameron completed his doctorate in 2015, titled "Cognitive Behavioural Therapy, Mindfulness-Based Interventions, and Heterogeneity Within Problem Gambling Samples: First Steps Towards Targeted Treatment in a Clinical Population." He has published work from the above thesis and on worry exposure for generalized anxiety disorder. Prior to his current career, Cameron held a number of managerial positions in international professional services, telecommunications, and retail corporations.

Katy O'Neill, PhD, MPsych (Clinical) is a clinical psychologist specializing in treating addictions including problem gambling. She has worked for 10 years at St Vincent's Hospital Gambling Treatment Program in Sydney. Prior to that, for over 20 years, she worked in drug, alcohol, and gambling outpatient services in a number of public hospitals. She has also supervised clinical psychologists in training clinics at the University of New South Wales and University of Sydney.

Chapter 1
Problem Gambling Treatment Background

Cameron McIntosh

Problem gambling (PG) is a significant public health concern (Gainsbury et al. 2013), and with greater opportunities to gamble provided by the relaxation of legislation regulating gambling in some countries over the last 25 years (Productivity Commission 2010), gambling behaviour is likely to at least remain at current levels in the near term. Gambling behaviour varies across populations and countries, with the estimated prevalence of the broadly defined and variously described 'problematic' or 'problem gambling' (PG) ranging from 0.15% in Norway to 5.3% in Hong Kong. PG prevalence rates of 2.1–3.1% (Hodgins et al. 2011) and 1.9–3.1% (Productivity Commission 2010) have been reported in the United States and Australia, respectively.

Disordered gambling is a recognised mental health condition that involves difficulty limiting gambling expenditure, lying about gambling and chasing losses (American Psychiatric Association [APA] 2013). Some of the consequences of PG are significant financial and psychological harm (Battersby and Tolchard 1996), with those engaging in PG also experiencing depression, self-harm, anxiety and engagement in other behaviours that compromise their well-being (Rodda and Cowie 2005; Delfabbro and LeCouteur 2009). PG has also been connected to poor employment outcomes, including taking time off and/or giving up work to gamble, job losses due to gambling or workplace criminal activities to fund gambling (Delfabbro and LeCouteur 2009).

The disproportionate negative effect that PG can have on vulnerable groups in communities is evidenced in estimates that PGs account for around 40% of the total gaming machine losses in Australia which is the predominant form of PG

C. McIntosh (✉)
St Vincent's Hospital Gambling Treatment Program, St Vincent's Hospital,
390 Victoria St, Darlinghurst, Sydney, NSW 2010, Australia
e-mail: cameron@uniqueminds.com.au

C. McIntosh, K. O'Neill, *Evidence-Based Treatments for Problem Gambling*,
SpringerBriefs in Psychology, DOI 10.1007/978-3-319-62485-3_1

(Productivity Commission 2010). The harm outlined above is possibly an understatement, as each individual engaged in PG can create physical, social and economic problems in 5–10 other individuals (Productivity Commission 1999).

As indicated above, considered examinations of PGs have reported extensive damage. Despite this severity PG treatment is based upon an outcome literature containing important methodological limitations (Ladouceur et al. 2003; National Centre for Education and Training on Addiction 2000; Toneatto and Ladouceur 2003). A number of these limitations can be attributed to the use of a broad range of terms to define PG, no unifying theory of how and why PG develops, the assumption that PGs are a homogeneous group in the treatment literature and a dearth of well-designed randomised controlled trials (RCTs) testing treatment interventions for this population.

Issues of Definition in PG Research

Terms used to describe PG include pathological, compulsive, disordered, level 2 and 3, at risk, problem, excessive, addicted and neurotic (APA 2004; Blaszczynski 2005; Blaszczynski and Nower 2002; National Research Council 1999; Petry 2005; Shaffer et al. 1997). The primary focus of these definitions has been to differentiate between controlled, recreational and social gambling and behaviour that causes significant harm to the gambling individual or others (Blaszczynski and Nower 2002). Implicit in the above definitions is the notion that PG behaviour can be categorised on a continuum of gambling-related harms (PGRTC 2011).

The difficulties in conceptualising PG are reflected in the history of gambling in the various iterations of the *Diagnostic and Statistics Manual of Mental Disorders* (DSM). At the more severe end of the continuum are the clinical definitions of gambling behaviour that reside in the DSM. Within the two most recent editions of the DSM, Fourth Edition-Text Revision (IV-TR) and Fifth Edition (5) (APA 2004, 2013), the criteria that established a clinically diagnosable gambling problem moved from the 'Impulse Control Disorders - Not Elsewhere Specified' to the 'Addiction and Related Disorders' sections in DSM-V. The recent changes in the DSM suggest a preference for conceptualising substance and behavioural addictions similarly; they emphasise the experience of the individual rather than the object of their addiction, and they enhance the approach of translating effective treatments from the substance use and misuse literature to PG treatment. The title of the disorder also changed from 'pathological gambling' to 'gambling disorder' in the DSM-V.

The clinical and dichotomously determined form of PG outlined above is distinct from the more broadly defined and commonly used term 'problem gambling'. The latter term incorporates the less severe end of the PG continuum. PG includes both clinical and subclinical gamblers, with the most broadly accepted definition in

Australia (PGRTC 2011) being provided by the Canadian Problem Gambling Index (Ferris and Wynne 2001):

> Problem gambling is characterized by difficulties in limiting money and/or time spent on gambling which leads to adverse consequences for the gambler, others, or for the community.

Within this book the terms 'problematic gambling' (PG) and 'problematic gamblers' (PGs) are used to describe the full continuum of PG as defined above. 'Gambling disorder' and 'pathological gambling' are used to describe the clinically diagnosable DSM conditions.

The Heterogeneity of Problem Gamblers

Leading researchers have stated that the heterogeneity within the PG population is evident (Blaszczynski 1999; Petry 2005), yet published gambling treatment research has tended to assume the homogeneity of participants on at least some of the diverse characteristics. The practice of defining PGs using subjective criteria has expanded the population of potential affected individuals, resulting in increased type I errors (Blaszczynski and Nower 2002). Whilst the broader approach may assist in identifying subclinical individuals for early intervention, it confuses concepts of gambling problems and clinical gambling problems and has led to contradictory and confusing results and difficulty in defining best practice (Blaszczynski and Nower 2002).

Examples of the heterogeneity within the PG population include clinical versus subclinical presentations of PG; differing levels at which individuals experience 'harm', for example, money lost gambling differs according to the socio-economic status of the individual; individuals seeking treatment appear to differ from those who do not seek treatment (Nettle 2007); the presence or absence of psychological dysfunction comorbid with the individual's PG, such as a mood disorder or attention deficit hyperactivity disorder (Petry 2005); individuals who meet the criteria for gambling disorder or pathological gambling have reported using a variety of forms of gambling in isolation or in combination, such as electronic gaming machines (EGMs), track betting and the more recently available sports betting; and the methods used by PGs to place bets can vary, for example, online versus in person at venues.

The subtyping models that have been recently developed for PGs vary on the constructs and techniques used to organise the participants studied. Some examples of the subtyping models include the pathways model which clustered PGs using theoretical pathways followed during the development of a gambling problem (Blaszczynski and Nower 2002), whilst another model clustered individuals using the degree of psychopathology expressed (Álvarez-Moya et al. 2010), and yet another used personality profiles (Vachon and Bagby 2009). The primary motivation for the establishment of agreed subtypes of PGs is that targeted treatments for the different subtypes of PGs are believed to improve treatment outcomes (Blaszczynski and Nower 2002; Milosevic and Ledgerwood 2010; Álvarez-Moya et al. 2010; Vachon and Bagby 2009; and Ledgerwood and Petry 2006).

Models of PG

People are motivated to gamble recreationally by the desire for arousal and excitement and relief from stress and negative mood (Rickwood et al. 2010). Knowledge of the factors that affect gambling participation across the lifespan is quite limited. There is also no widely accepted causal explanation or single theoretical model that adequately accounts for the aetiology of PG (Rickwood et al. 2010). Learning theory, cognitive models and neurophysiological models all have some evidence base. Very little evidence supports personality or psychoanalytic explanations (Rickwood et al. 2010). Integrated models comprising bio-psychosocial and pathways approaches are supported by emerging evidence, consistent with the aetiology of other psychological and substance misuse disorders.

Examples of models that have been developed to describe PG are the pathways model (Blaszczynski and Nower 2002) and cognitive behavioural approaches (Sharpe and Tarrier 1993; Sharpe 2002; Raylu and Oei 2010). The pathways model sets out at least three primary subgroups of gamblers: behaviourally conditioned, emotionally vulnerable and biologically based impulsive pathways into PG. The CBT model for PG is consistent with those of other psychological disorders, where genes and environment of the individual, personality traits, the occurrence of irrational and negative cognitions, negative psychological states and sociological factors (Raylu and Oei 2010) are all relevant.

Brief Summary of Treatment Outcomes for Problem Gamblers

Treatment of PG has tended to focus at the public health and/or clinical level. A community and public health perspective of PG supports a harm minimisation approach (Dickerson 2003). Although hampered by the lack of an operational definition of harm, this approach focusses on risk and protective factors to prevent and reduce gambling harm. Primary prevention approaches have generally relied on educational campaigns to increase knowledge, although these are yet to be demonstrated empirically to be effective in achieving subsequent behaviour change. Secondary prevention approaches address individuals at higher risk and comprise policy initiatives, such as gambling venue staff training, and modifications to gambling environments and restricting access to cash.

Clinical research and individual treatment for PG, which is the focus of this book, face a number of challenges such as the impact of monetary incentives to participate, difficulty in subject recruitment, treatment ambivalence, the role of natural recovery, the impact of intractable financial pressures and the specification of adequate process and outcome measures (Toneatto 2005). Further difficulties in ameliorating the impacts of disordered gambling arise as less than 10% of PGs seek formal treatment (Cunningham 2005; Slutske 2006), and treatment dropout rates are in the vicinity of 50% (Melville et al. 2007; Ladouceur et al. 2001). Consequently, there is a clear need for the examination of effective assessment, screening, improved treatment continuation, reducing treatment barriers as well as improving the effectiveness and breadth of treatment therapies for PGs based upon well-designed research.

To date, the treatment for PG has included pharmacotherapy and psychological approaches. We have provided chapters on both of these approaches, with an emphasis on the latter. The psychological approaches reported in the treatment literature include psychoanalytic/psychodynamic therapy, '12-step' gamblers anonymous programmes, cognitive behavioural therapy (CBT), motivational interviewing, self-help manuals and combined or dismantled versions of the preceding types of therapy (PGRTC 2011). Mindfulness-based interventions have begun to be examined recently also (McIntosh et al. 2016).

In line with the improvements needed in treating PG outlined above, a recent systematic review described the current evidence base supporting the assessment, screening and treatment therapies for PGs as 'immature' (PGRTC 2011). At present, the psychological treatments reported to be used for PG have varying levels of evidence (PGRTC). CBT is currently deemed to be the most effective treatment for PG, although CBT only received a 'cautious' recommendation for use with PGs from the PGRTC review. The effectiveness of the predominant contemporary interventions, including those that are gaining clinician support but not yet research endorsement for PG, is the focus of this book.

Transdiagnostic Conceptualisation of PG Treatment

A transdiagnostic conceptualisation promotes the development of unified treatment protocols that emphasise commonalities across a range of disorders, rather than identifying differences between disorders and encouraging specialisation of different treatment modalities (Mcevoy and Nathan 2007). One advantage of this approach is that the impact of the respective treatments on the underlying processes maintaining the dysfunction prior to treatment can be examined, and an initial transdiagnostic conceptualisation of treatment for PG may be applicable. An advantage of conceptualising an effective treatment from a transdiagnostic perspective is that the transdiagnostic treatment format is particularly conducive to dissemination into service provision settings and has the potential to treat comorbidities in an effective way without compromising the primary treatment targets. The transdiagnostic approach may introduce flexibility into manualised treatments, offer greater allowance for heterogeneous clinical presentations and provide a balance between flexibility and fidelity that maximises both (McHugh et al. 2009). Although transdiagnostic interventions have not been applied to PG samples in research that has been reported to date, they do appear to offer benefits that would justify further investigation.

Defining the Problems Addressed in Book

The International Gambling Think Tank (IGTT) consists of the world's leading scientists in gambling and addiction from the United States, Canada, the European Union, the UK, the Nordic countries, Asia, Australia and New Zealand. The IGTT endorsed the publication of the systematic review by the PGRTC (2011), which outlined the state of knowledge concerning the screening, assessment and treatment practices of PG. Of concern, the review was only able to identify a few 'evidenced-based recommendations' to guide the treatment of PGs due to the paucity of findings meeting the PGRTC's criteria in the literature.

To address the above concern, the PGRTC (2011) provided a number of recommendations for further research in this area. The recommendations included conducting randomised controlled trials (RCTs) into the effectiveness of CBT and psychological interventions other than CBT and comparing outcomes between treatments. The PGRTC also recommended that future research into treatment efficacy should account for heterogeneity within the PG population and that gambling behaviour and severity, psychological distress, alcohol and substance misuse and quality of life measures be used wherever possible to increase the validity of research and improve treatment guidance.

There are a number of other factors surrounding PG and its treatment that make this such a fertile area within which to advance the discussion of contemporary treatment options. Some examples include the various training backgrounds of clinicians practising in this area, funding of treatment services and the fidelity of the delivery of the interventions. Funding models for PG treatment range from government-provided free services subsidised via taxes on certain operators in the gambling industry, for example, casinos in Australia, to full private funding by the PG, possibly including rebates via government health systems. In Australia this has meant that clinicians' backgrounds can range from counselling to clinical psychologists to psychiatrists reducing the consistency of the way treatment is conceptualised, operationalised and reported. Whilst diversity of the clinicians' backgrounds can be a strength for treatment development for the PG population, it can mean that 'eclectic' treatments are delivered and that research and development can be compromised if outcomes remain anecdotal or methodologies are not clearly articulated when results are shared.

This book seeks to contribute to the discussion of contemporary treatments of PG by examining CBT and alternative treatments for PG to address the 'immature' status of the treatment literature for this population. With less than 10% of PGs seeking formal treatment (Cunningham 2005; Slutske 2006) and treatment dropout rates in the vicinity of 50% (Melville et al. 2007; Ladouceur et al. 2001), alternative treatments that may improve these statistics are warranted. The overarching aim of this book is to promote the focus on evidenced-based interventions for clinicians treating PG, to provide insight into the gaps in the research literature for PGs and ultimately to improve treatment outcomes.

References

Álvarez-Moya, E. M., Jiménez-Murcia, S., Aymamí, N. A., et al. (2010). Sub-typing study of a pathological gamblers sample. *La Revue canadiennede psychiatrie, 55*(8), 498–406.

American Psychiatric Association. (2004). *Diagnostic and statistical manual of mental disorders: Text revision* (4th ed rev ed.). Washington, DC: American Psychiatric Association.

American Psychiatric Association. (2013). *Diagnostic and statistical manual of mental disorder* (5th ed.). Washington, DC: American Psychiatric Association.

Battersby, M., & Tolchard, B. (1996). The effect of treatment of pathological gamblers referred to a behavioural psychotherapy unit: II – Outcome of three kinds of behavioural intervention. In B. Tolchard (Ed.). *Towards 2000: The future of gambling: Proceedings of the 7th annual conference of the National Association for Gambling Studies* (pp. 219–227), Adelaide.

Blaszczynski, A. (1999). Pathological gambling: An impulse control, addictive or obsessive–compulsive disorder? *Anuario de Psicologia, 30*, 93–109.

Blaszczynski, A. (2005). How to treat problem gambling: *Australian Doctor*, 12 August, 37–44.

Blaszczynski, A., & Nower, L. (2002). A pathways model for problem and pathological gambling. *Addiction, 97*(5), 487–499.

Cunningham, J. A. (2005). Little use of treatment among problem gamblers. *Psychiatry Services, 56*, 1024–1025.

Delfabbro, P. H., & LeCouteur, A. L. (2009). *Australasian gambling review* (4th ed.). Adelaide: Independent Gambling Authority of South Australia.

Dickerson, M. (2003). Exploring the limits of 'Responsible Gambling': Harm minimisation or consumer protection? *Proceedings of the 12th annual conference of the national association for gambling studies*, Melbourne.

Ferris, J., & Wynne, H. (2001). *The Canadian problem gambling index*. Ottawa: Canadian Centre on Substance Abuse.

Gainsbury, S. M., Blankers, M., Wilkinson, C., Schelleman-Offermans, K., & Cousijn, J. (2013). Recommendations for international gambling harm-minimisation guidelines: Comparison with effective public health policy. *Journal of Gambling Studies, 30*(4), 771–788.

Hodgins, D. C., Stea, J. N., & Grant, J. N. (2011). Gambling disorders. *Lancet, 378*, 1874–1884.

Ladouceur, R., Gosselin, P., Laberge, M., & Blaszczynski, A. (2001). Dropouts in clinical research: Do results reported in the field of addiction reflect clinical reality? *The Behavior Therapist, 24*, 44–46.

Ladouceur, R., Sylvain, C., Boutin, C., Lachance, S., Doucet, C., & Leblond, J. (2003). Group therapy for pathological gamblers: A cognitive approach. *Behaviour Research and Therapy, 41*, 587–596.

Ledgerwood, D. M., & Petry, N. M. (2006). Psychological experience of gambling and subtypes of pathological gamblers. *Psychiatry Research, 144*(1), 17–27.

Mcevoy, P. M., & Nathan, P. (2007). Effectiveness of cognitive behavior therapy for diagnostically heterogeneous groups: A benchmarking study. *Journal of Consulting and Clinical Psychology, 75*(2), 344–350.

McHugh, K., Murray, H. W., & Barlow, D. H. (2009). Balancing fidelity and adaptation in the dissemination of empirically-supported treatments: The promise of transdiagnostic interventions. *Behaviour Research and Therapy, 47*(11), 946–953.

McIntosh, C. C., Crino, R. D., & O'Neill, K. (2016). Treating problem gambling samples with cognitive behavioural therapy and mindfulness-based interventions: A clinical trial. *Journal of Gambling Studies, 32*, 1305–1325. doi:10.1007/s10899-016-9602-1.

Melville, K. M., Casey, L. M., & Kavanagh, D. J. (2007). Psychological treatment dropout among pathological gamblers. *Clinical Psychology Review, 27*, 944–958.

Milosevic, A., & Ledgerwood, D. M. (2010). The sub-typing of pathological gambling: A comprehensive review. *Clinical Psychology Review, 30*, 988–998.

National Centre for Education and Training on Addiction [NCETA]. (2000). *Current "best practice" interventions for gambling problems: A theoretical and empirical review*. Melbourne: Victorian Government Department of Human Services.

National Research Council. (1999). *Pathological gambling: A critical review*. Washington, DC: National Academy Press.

Nettle, D. (2007). *Personality*. United Kingdom: Oxford University Press.

Petry. (2005). *Pathological gambling: Etiology, comorbidity, and treatment*. USA: American Psychological Association.

Problem Gambling Research & Treatment Centre (2011). *Guideline for screening, assessment and treatment of problem gambling*. Clayton: Monash University.

Productivity Commission. (1999). *Australia's gambling industries*. Canberra: Productivity Commission.

Productivity Commission (2010). *Gambling. Productivity commission inquiry report. Volume 1. Report no. 50*. Canberra: Productivity Commission.

Raylu, N., & Oei, T. P. S. (2010). *A cognitive behavioural therapy programme for problem gambling: Therapist manual*. New York: Routledge.

Rickwood, D., Blaszczynski, A., Delfabbro, P., Dowling, N., Heading, K. (2010). The psychology of gambling APS review paper: Australian Psychological Society.

Rodda, S., & Cowie, M. (2005). *Evaluation of electronic gaming machine harm minimisation in Victoria*. Report prepared for the Victorian Department of Justice. Melbourne: Caraniche Pty. Ltd.

Shaffer, H.J., Hall, M.N., Vander Bilt, J. (1997). *Estimating the prevalence of disordered gambling in the United States and Canada: A meta-analysis*. Boston: Harvard Medical School, Division of Addictions. USA.

Sharpe, L. A. (2002). Reformulated cognitive-behavioral model of problem gambling: A biopsychosocial perspective. *Clinical Psychology Revue, 22*, 1–25.

Sharpe, L., & Tarrier, N. (1993). Towards a cognitive-behavioural theory of problem gambling. *British Journal of Psychiatry, 162*, 407–412.

Slutske, W. S. (2006). Natural recovery and treatment-seeking in pathological gambling: Results of two US national surveys. *American Journal of Psychiatry, 163*(2), 297–302.

Toneatto, T. (2005). A perspective on problem gambling treatment: Issues and challenges. *Journal of Gambling Studies, 21*(1), 73–78.

Toneatto, T., & Ladouceur, R. (2003). Treatment of pathological gambling: A critical review of the literature. *Psychology of Addictive Behaviours, 17*, 284–292.

Vachon, D. D., & Bagby, R. M. (2009). Pathological gambling sub-types. *Psychological Assessment, 21*, 608–615.

Chapter 2
Psychoeducation for Problem Gambling

Katy O'Neill

Problem gamblers are often deeply embarrassed, ashamed and mystified by their ongoing self-destructive behaviour. Indeed, bewilderment seems to be a feature of both those who experience problem gambling and those who study it. Two different authors writing decades apart both wrote books titled *The Psychology of Gambling*. Both express bewilderment from their very different perspectives.

"The gambler is apparently the last optimist. He is a creature totally unmoved by experience. His belief in ultimate success cannot be shattered by financial loss, however great. He did not win today? So what? Tomorrow will be lucky. He's lost again? It doesn't prove a thing: someday he's bound to win. Where logic ends, the unconscious takes over. His illogical senseless certainty that he will win is an unconscious attack on reality" Dr. Edmund Bergler (1957).

"Gambling behaviour is an enigma. It is an area of human behaviour that is full of paradoxes. Most of all, it is a challenge to our best theories of human nature. Nearly all gambling is structured so that the gambler should expect to lose, all things being equal. Some gamblers give up everything of value in their lives in order to gamble: family, properties, friends, self-esteem. Why should anyone give up so much in such a futile cause?" Dr. Michael Walker (1995).

Problem gamblers are often similarly bewildered. They ask themselves questions such as "Why don't I stop before I run out of money? Do I really want to destroy myself and my family?" Problem gamblers present to therapy already having formed their own theories. Unfortunately, their theories often involve an unchangeable, incomprehensible, inner flaw deep within. One can easily hear Seligman's three helplessness attributions in these explanations – personal, permanent and

K. O'Neill (✉)
St Vincent's Hospital Gambling Treatment Program, St Vincent's Hospital,
390 Victoria St, Darlinghurst, Sydney, NSW 2010, Australia
e-mail: ko@kogo.net.au

C. McIntosh, K. O'Neill, *Evidence-Based Treatments for Problem Gambling*,
SpringerBriefs in Psychology, DOI 10.1007/978-3-319-62485-3_2

pervasive (Seligman 1990). One of the aims of psychoeducation, therefore, is to open opportunities for intervention. Theoretical explanations, even if only ever partial accounts, that allow for change provide a rationale for treatment and help to counter demoralisation, shame and stigma.

Psychoeducation needs only take one session (a syllabus checklist may stop the client from feeling overwhelmed). To be memorable, psychoeducation should be presented using vivid examples as described below (e.g. the Stroop, Muller-Lyer illusion, the story of Ulysses).

Our All Too Human Minds

Over the past decade or so, the public imagination has engaged with the notion that human kind is not as rational and reasoned as we like to think ourselves. Recent popular books by academics include *Predictably Irrational* by Dan Ariely (2008), *The Invisible Gorilla and Other Ways Our Intuition Deceives Us* by Christopher Chabris and Daniel Simons (2010), *Brain Bugs: How the Brain's Flaws Shape Our Lives* by Dean Buonomano (2011) and even one by a magician, *Tricks of the Mind* by Derren Brown (2007). Perhaps the best known is *Thinking, Fast and Slow* by Nobel Prize winner Daniel Kahneman (2011).

There are many ways to illustrate that we can't always trust how or what we think. One easy way of suggesting that we can believe two contradictory things at once is the Muller-Lyer illusion. Draw two parallel lines of equal length. Measure them in front of your client. Then draw arrow heads on one line (as if the line represented an outside corner) and outward open-ended fins or "reverse" arrow heads on the other line (as if the line represented an inside corner). Now one line will look decidedly shorter than the other. This gives the client a sense of simultaneously believing two contradictory things (the lines are the same; the lines are different). This illusion can be used to vividly highlight the point that we can seemingly simultaneously hold two inconsistent beliefs despite our factual knowledge. In the case of gambling – a client may be simultaneously torn between thoughts about going gambling and thoughts about resisting the urge; thoughts acknowledging the possibility of losing while simultaneously believing one is on the verge of a big win.

Kahneman (2011) labelled two distinct ways of thinking. System 1 is automatic, quick and involuntary and uses heuristics. System 2 is effortful, slower and deliberate. The conclusion we want our problem gambling clients to draw is that these heuristics are very human and not unique to gamblers. All of us rely on them in situations of ambiguity, uncertainty and when under cognitive load. This means of course that some cognitive distortions are inherent in gambling (Petry 2005). This information should help the gambler have more scepticism towards any hunches they may feel as well as making them feel less foolish.

The Awesome Power of Intermittent Reinforcement Schedules

In the case of electronic gaming machines (EGMs), problem gamblers have unknowingly been subjected to powerful conditioning schedules; the strength of which can be judged by their financial losses and extent of their bewilderment. Informing our clients about relevant aspects of learning theory does not deny their individuality but affirms it. Behaviourist explanations of reinforcement schedules resonate with people struggling with their attraction to slot machines (Schull 2012).

Explaining intermittent reinforcement need not take long – especially if the client has ever had a pet. During continuous reinforcement rats learn that pressing the lever brings a food pellet. If the food stops, the rat will stop pressing, the response has been extinguished. However, if the rat has been reinforced intermittently when food stops, the rat will continue to respond. Knowing this helps the client appreciate one reason it is so hard to stop – their responses cannot be extinguished: they can never be sure that the next bet won't be a winner. Furthermore, the intermittent reinforcement in EGMs is highly variable, so unpredictable as to approximate randomness. If the reinforcement was on a fixed interval or a fixed ratio, then the rat (or gambler) could take a rest after certain periods of time or after a number of presses. But when the reinforcement is unpredictable, rests are avoided, rats press to exhaustion, and similarly, players avoid leaving their machines.

What Urges Do and Don't Mean

Kavanagh et al. (2004) note that one of the most distressing aspects of urges during attempted abstinence concerns the meaning of the urge. Gamblers worry that perhaps it means they can never gain control or that relapse is imminent (Marlatt and Parks 1982). In motivational interviewing Miller and Rollnick (1991) reframe the meaning of alcohol tolerance from "I can handle my drinks so it doesn't hurt me" to "drinking could be harming my health without me noticing the effects". Urges can be helpfully reframed as a sign that the urge is felt because the habit is fading; an urge is a conditioned response and a natural part of extinction and not a sign of personal weakness (Marlatt and Parks 1982).

Practice Makes Too Perfect

Bargh and Chartrand (1999) cite research indicating that a wide range of mental processes and behaviours can unintentionally or intentionally become automatic and cued outside conscious awareness. Using the Stroop paradigm can illustrate the effort necessary to inhibit such well-learned responses. Provide a list of colours, written in the same colour as the word, e.g. RED is written in red ink, BLUE in blue, and GREEN in green. Ask the client to identify the colour instead of the content of the word. This is easy. Then provide a second list in which the words are printed in non-matching colours, e.g. RED is printed in blue ink, BLUE is printed in green ink, GREEN is printed in red ink, etc. Again, ask the client to identify the colour instead of the word. Most people find themselves stumbling when they need to inhibit the overlearned response of reading the word. This is due to repetition making the reading of words automatic. Gamblers have undergone an amount of repetition which would please any music or language or sports teacher.

Unfortunately, the automaticity persists, rather like the aphorism that something is like learning to ride a bicycle – having learned to ride a bicycle in one's childhood, one is quicker to pick it up again than if one had never learned. A skill that has not been utilised for many years does not vanish altogether but lies dormant until the cues are present. Anecdotes exist of Australian gamblers who lived overseas in jurisdictions without poker machines for many years and didn't miss them at all, only to relapse when back in Australia.

The implication that one has developed a habit which is long lasting and potentially lies dormant can be discouraging. The point is not to be discouraged but to appreciate that learning new habits in response to the old triggers may take a lot of repetition and awareness. New habits of course can be learned. The folk wisdom that weeks of meditation change your brain and other examples of neuroplasticity can provide hope.

When the Thrill of the Chase Is Never Ending: Affective Neuroscience

Zack (2006) asserts that the field of affective neuroscience can teach us a great deal about gambling. Panksepp, a pioneer of the field, argues that "various environmental challenges were so persistent during brain evolution that psycho-behavioural tendencies to respond to such challenges have been encoded as neural circuits within the mammalian brain" (1998 page 50). One such circuit is the SEEKING system. Rats don't need to be taught to forage, nor do dogs need to be taught to follow a scent. Similarly, humans seek to understand, to play and to discover. The SEEKING system is accompanied by desire, hope, anticipation, stimulus-bound appetitive behaviour (adjunctive behaviours) and occasionally superstitious behaviour (Panksepp 1998).

The SEEKING system is predominantly mediated by dopamine. The dopamine system responds selectively to novel, attention-grabbing events and stimuli that predict reward. The incentive sensitization theory of addiction posits that dopamine accompanies reward (experienced as pleasure) but that it also responds to cues that signal the possibility of reward (experienced as motivation) (Robinson and Berridge 2000). Furthermore, the cues of a possible reward trigger fluctuations in levels of dopamine. Schultz et al. 1997 established that dopamine is a neural substrate of prediction and reward, making dopamine particularly relevant in problem gambling.

Using functional magnetic resonance imaging (fMRI), Clark et al. (2009) showed that near misses were felt to be less pleasant but more motivating, leading to an increased desire to play due to "an anomalous recruitment of reward circuitry" (Clark et al. 2009).

Zack (2006) also notes that with respect to the SEEKING system, gambling withdrawal would be expected to involve feelings of boredom or restlessness, an uncomfortable state of disengagement with the world. This must be what Blaise Pascal intuitively understood when he invented the roulette wheel. He wrote that people seek *divertissement* from their chronic state of *ennui* (i.e. to be distracted from the anxious emptiness of our lives) (Pascal 1966). Spinella (2003) suggests that pathological gambling is an example of evolutionary mismatch. A more familiar example is how our innate taste for sugar, fat and salt have not served us well in an environment of easily available food. Similarly, Spinella suggests, a whole range of survival skills have been hijacked in modern gambling environments. Persistence, risk-taking, preference for novelty, hope and getting over losses quickly can be advantageous in other contexts. The gaming environment of gambling is artificially unpredictable yet evokes our human inclination to search for patterns and try to learn from previous outcomes.

An explanation of some of the neurobiology that underlies the desire to continue to gamble despite one's best interests helps clients take a step back from such feelings and understand them in an environmental context as well as reducing shame.

Electronic Gaming Machines

Most treatment-seeking gamblers prefer electronic gaming machines (EGMs) (Hodgins et al. 2001). Natasha Schull in her 2012 book *Addiction by Design* describes in fascinating detail how various design features of EGMs are deliberately geared towards extending "time on device". Turner and Horbay (2004) suggest that poker machines or slots (EGMs) take players beyond the limits of human reasoning. They provide an excellent guide to the inner workings of EGMs in the *Journal of Gambling Issues* 2004 volume 10. Available free online at http://jgi.camh.net/doi/full/10.4309/jgi.2004.11.21. They also suggest that EGMs are the most misunderstood of all forms of gambling. Frequently asked questions often centre on random number generators.

A random number generator (RNG) uses a complex algorithm – for example, starting with a seed number such as the time of day and then multiplying, adding and dividing by very large numbers to arrive at a number – the remainder of which is the first random number and the next seed number. Technically RNG generates numbers that are not random but pseudorandom. It could take billions of samples to repeat the cycle. To further increase the impossibility of predicting the cycle, the RNG runs continuously once the machine is turned on, even if no one is playing it. A press by a player merely samples the random number generated at that moment, so a player could never know which part of the cycle they are in. Furthermore, the pictures shown on a slot reel do not necessarily correspond directly to the odds of winning. A symbol might occur twice on the reel but only land on the payline once every 50 spins. This is accomplished through a process called virtual mapping. Each stop on the slot machine's "virtual" reel is equally likely, but more of these virtual reel stops are mapped onto low or non-paying symbols than onto high-paying symbols.

The players information booklet from none other than the Australian Association of Gaming Machine Manufacturers (now Gaming Technologies Australia) explains: "If a King symbol is assigned to positions 1,4,13,18,22, and 31 that assignment is permanent, it does not change from game to game.... It may be, and this is often the case, that the jackpot symbol is only assigned to one stopping position on the wheel so the chances of getting 5 symbols may be as low as one in 52.5 million". Schull (2012) notes that in legal disputes about the programming of near misses, manufacturers argue that since the source of near misses lies in the reels' configuration prior to a spin, and not in secondary software after a spin, near misses are not programmed in response to player activity.

Mathematics and Probability

Kahneman (2011) says we humans tend to see patterns where none exist and show "serious mistakes in evaluating the randomness of random events" (page 115). Turner found that problem gamblers have a poorer understanding of randomness (Turner and Liu 1999; cited in Turner 2002). For example, problem gamblers were more likely to believe that betting on a number that looks random gives you a better chance of winning. Turner explains "Random numbers don't necessarily look random". A ticket with the numbers 1 – 2 – 3 – 4 – 5 – 6 has the same chance of winning as a ticket with the numbers 3 – 17 – 21 – 28 – 32 – 47, but many people have trouble believing this. Most of the time random numbers look random. Problem gamblers often do not appreciate independence of turns. Turner suggests that what fools many people into believing that randomness is self-correcting stems from our experiences of witnessing regression to the mean. He explains that on average a coin comes up heads 50% of the time. Even if heads come up 1000 times in a row, the next flip could be a head or a tail. If a coin flip is truly random, then it must be possible (although very unlikely) for it to come up heads 1 million times in a row. The number of heads and tails does not have to even out. A head is just as likely to occur after five heads as after five tails. The more flips you make, the closer the average gets to 50%, but nothing can force it to even out.

Turner (2002) concludes "The human mind is not very good at dealing with randomness. Our minds are designed to find order, not to appreciate chaos. We are wired to look for patterns and find connections, and when we find patterns we interpret them as real. Consequently, many people will see patterns in random numbers. When people see patterns in randomness (e.g. repeated numbers, apparent sequences or winning streaks) they may believe that the numbers aren't truly random, and therefore, can be predicted".

Ulysses: A Metacognitive Hero!

In Greek mythology, the sirens were creatures (half woman, half bird) who lured sailors to their deaths. The sirens' song was so sweet that sailors were unable to resist and would steer their boats into the rocks and perish. The term "siren song" now refers to an attraction that is hard to resist but if heeded will lead to a bad result.

Ulysses knew he had to pass the sirens' island to get home to his wife Penelope. He might have relied on sheer willpower and the strength of his motivation to get home and simply made a resolution to be strong when he heard their song. This would have arrogantly assumed that in the same situation, he would act differently to all those sailors who had been caught before him. Ulysses, however, was wiser than that. Ulysses understood human nature and knew that strength and motivation ebb and flow and that even the most committed can waver in the face of temptation. So he put wax in his crews' ears and tied himself to the mast. Although he begged to be untied when he heard the Siren song, his crew could not hear him or the sirens, and they all sailed out of danger.

In a dry retelling of this tale, Ross et al. (2008) say "Notice that Ulysses thereby showed awareness of his own disposition for inter-temporal preference reversal and used this foreknowledge to block its dangers" (page 66).

The Ulysses story contains many analogues to clinically useful insights and strategies. Ulysses is motivated by a meaningful goal, his family relationships and to get home; he wants to reunite with his wife Penelope. He did not blindly trust that the strength of his current motivation to get home would endure through the future high-risk situation of hearing the sirens' song. He understood that motivation is not a fixed state – it is susceptible to environmental influences – our beliefs are somewhat state dependent and can change. He knew motivation was not enough; he needed planning and strategy. He undertook a functional analysis of his high-risk situation. He used a range of creative strategies, wax to prevent the crew from hearing the song (stimulus control) and rope to tie himself to the mast to prevent himself from responding.

Ulysses and the sirens is a good metaphor for dealing with cravings that we cannot avoid. Ulysses shows a lot of wisdom – sophisticated self-awareness, practical compassion and cunning strategy rather than blind hope. What these days could be called metacognitive insight! He adopts strategies which mirror behavioural strategies such as stimulus control and alternative behaviours as recommended for the early stage of treatment in a number of contemporary manuals: For example, identify high-risk times; bind up access to money; schedule alternate non-gambling activities, especially for those times one would be at a loose end without gambling; and arrange to get together with friends and family (see, e.g. Petry 2005; Ladouceur and Lachance 2007; Raylu and Oei 2010).

In practice, clients can tie themselves to a metaphorical mast in all sorts of creative ways. For example, to avoid the risky period after work, a client can ring home before leaving work, "I'll be home soon – do you want me to get milk or bread on the way home?" Soon this will become an expected daily routine and thoughts like

"I'll only pop in for half an hour and no one will know" will no longer occur. The partner may not even realise the problem gambler has been tying him or herself to the mast.

With insight, self-awareness and a little forward planning like Ulysses, problem gamblers can set things up now (while motivated) so that they can resist when temptation strikes in the future.

References

Ariely, D. (2008). *Predictably irrational: The hidden forces that shape our decisions*. London: HarperCollins Publishers.

Bargh, J. A., & Chartrand, T. L. (1999). The unbearable automaticity of being. *American Psychologist, 54*, 452–479.

Bergler, E. (1957). *The psychology of gambling*. New York: Hill and Wang.

Brown, D. (2007). *Tricks of the mind*. London: Transworld Publishers.

Buonomano, D. (2011). *Brain bugs: How the brain's flaws shape our lives*. New York: W.W. Norton and Company.

Chabris, C., & Simons, D. (2010). *The invisible gorilla and other ways our intuition deceives us*. London: HarperCollins Publishers.

Clark, L., Lawrence, A. J., Astley-Jones, F., & Gray, N. (2009). Gambling near-misses enhance motivation to gamble and recruit win-related brain circuitry. *Neuron, 61*, 481–490. doi:10.1016/j.neuron.2008.12.031.

Gaming Technologies Australia (formerly Australian Gaming Machine Manufacturers Association) *Australian gaming machines player information booklet.*

Hodgins, D. C., Currie, S. R., & el-Guebaly, N. (2001). *Motivational enhancement* and self-help treatments for problem gambling. *Journal of Consulting and Clinical Psychology, 69*(1), 50–57.

Kahneman, D. (2011). *Thinking, fast and slow*. London: Penguin Books.

Kavanagh, D. J., Andrade, J., & May, J. (2004). Beating the urge: Implications of research into substance-related desires. *Addictive Behaviors, 29*, 1359–1372. doi:10.1016/j.addbeh.2004.06.009.

Ladouceur, R., & Lachance, S. (2007). *Overcoming pathological gambling: Therapist guide*. Oxford: Oxford University Press.

Marlatt, G. A., & Parks, G. A. (1982). Self-management of addictive behaviors. In P. Karoly & F. H. Kanfer (Eds.), *Self-management and behaviour change*. New York: Pergamon Press.

Miller, W. R., & Rollnick, S. (1991). *Motivational interviewing: Preparing people to change addictive behaviour*. New York: The Guilford Press.

Panksepp, J. (1998). *Affective neuroscience: The foundations of human and animal emotions*. Oxford: Oxford University Press.

Pascal, B. (1966). *Human happiness*. London: Penguin Books edition.

Petry, N. M. (2005). *Pathological gambling: Etiology, comorbidity, and treatment*. Washington: American Psychological Association.

Raylu, N., & Oei, T. P. (2010). *A cognitive behavioural therapy programme for problem gambling: Therapist manual*. London: Routledge.

Robinson, T. E., & Berridge, K. C. (2000). The psychology and neurobiology of addiction: An incentive-sensitization view. *Addiction, 95*(Supplement 2), S91–S117.

Ross, D., Sharp, C., Vuchinich, R. E., & Spurrett, D. (2008). *Midbrain mutiny: The picoeconomics and neuroeconomics of disordered gambling*. Massachusetts: MIT Press.

Schull, N. D. (2012). *Addiction by design: Machine gambling in Las Vegas*. Princeton NJ: Princeton University Press.

Schultz, W., Dayan, P., & Montague, P. R. (1997). A neural substrate of prediction and reward. *Science, 275*, 1593–1599.

Seligman, M. E. P. (1990). *Learned optimism*. Sydney: Random House Australia.

Spinella, M. (2003). Evolutionary mismatch, neural reward circuits, and pathological gambling. *International Journal of Neuroscience, 113*, 503–512. doi:10.1080/00207450390162254.

Turner, N. (2002). Randomness, does it matter? *Journal of Gambling Issues, 2*. doi:10.4309/jgi.2002.6.2.

Turner, N., & Horbay, R. (2004). How do slot machines and other electronic gambling machines actually work? *Journal of Gambling Issues, 11*. doi:10.4309/jgi.2006.17.7.

Walker, M. B. (1995). *The psychology of gambling*. Oxford: Pergamon Press.

Zack, M. (2006). What can affective neuroscience teach us about gambling? *Journal of Gambling Issues, 16*. doi:10.4309/jgi.2006.16.20.

Chapter 3
Motivational Interviewing for Problem Gambling

Katy O'Neill

In their first edition of Motivational Interviewing (MI), Miller and Rollnick (1991) deliberately avoided providing a definition of MI. Later they offered the following definition: MI is a client-centred, directive method for enhancing intrinsic motivation to change by exploring and resolving ambivalence (Miller and Rollnick 2002). Miller and Rollnick (2013) went on to clarify what MI is not. In particular they noted that MI differs from the client-centred counselling approach of Carl Rogers by being deliberately and consciously directive. The interviewer elicits and selectively reinforces change talk (see below). Initially developed to prepare ambivalent substance using clients for treatment, MI went on to become a treatment in its own right for helping to resolve ambivalence in a range of disorders (Miller and Rollnick 1991, 2002, 2013; Arkowitz et al. 2008).

Mechanisms of Change in MI

For an intervention with so much evidence of efficacy (there have been over 200 randomised controlled trials – see Miller and Rollnick 2013 for a list), it comes as somewhat of a surprise that the mechanisms of MI are still a matter of conjecture.

Diskin and Hodgins (2009) explained the efficacy of MI compared to a control interview. The control interview was largely a personality assessment designed to control for time with a therapist. At 1-year follow-up, both groups had reduced gambling, but the MI group had reduced gambling significantly more than the control interview group. Diskin and Hodgins suggested that, most importantly, it is the

K. O'Neill (✉)
St Vincent's Hospital Gambling Treatment Program, St Vincent's Hospital,
390 Victoria St, Darlinghurst, Sydney, NSW 2010, Australia
e-mail: ko@kogo.net.au

C. McIntosh, K. O'Neill, *Evidence-Based Treatments for Problem Gambling*,
SpringerBriefs in Psychology, DOI 10.1007/978-3-319-62485-3_3

willingness of the therapist to acknowledge and accept gamblers' ambivalence about the possibility of changing their behaviour. Rather than demanding a firm commitment for change, coupled with a complete rejection of "the good things" that gambling is perceived to provide, the interviews encouraged participants to talk about both the positive and negative aspects of their gambling behaviour. Diskin and Hodgins noted that the MI interviews provided an opportunity for participants to explore their values, to think about the future and to think about the people and principles they held dear. They wrote that these discussions were often "emotionally charged interactions in which the interviewer played a supportive and non-judgemental role, allowing participants to express and acknowledge their [mixed] feelings about their behaviour and to imagine the possibility of change" (Diskin and Hodgins 2009, page 387).

Miller and Rose (2009) proposed that MI worked through two strands – one is the therapeutic relationship itself, and the other is the evoking of inner motivation through the eliciting of "change talk". Certainly the relationship is crucial. Jones et al. (2015) studied the client experience of MI. Clients watched a videotape of their MI session and were asked to identify and describe the important moments in the therapy session. The transcribed interviews were then analysed using grounded theory. The aspects of therapy which clients felt were important were consistent with the theoretical aims of MI and included a non confrontational approach, affirmation, developing discrepancies between beliefs and behaviour and maintaining autonomy.

Descriptions of the ideals of MI are contained in studies that attempt to understand the mechanisms of change in MI. Such studies code therapist behaviours as either consistent or inconsistent with MI. Therapist behaviours that are consistent with the MI spirit include collaboration, evoking the client's ideas about change and autonomy, the use of reflection, open questions, affirming (Copeland et al. 2015) or empathy, acceptance, warmth and genuineness (Apodaca and Longabaugh 2009). Therapist behaviours that are inconsistent with MI include confronting, warning and giving advice without permission.

Westra and Dozois (2008) integrate MI into the treatment of anxiety. They note that the decisional balance, done either explicitly or implicitly, is the main framework that guides their work with ambivalence. In a meta-analysis of MI components, the decisional balance was the component with the strongest association with better outcomes (Apodaca and Longabaugh 2009).

General Principles of MI

In their first manual of MI (1991), Miller and Rollnick listed five general principles of MI which they named alliteratively. These principles were to Express Empathy, Develop Discrepancy, Avoid Argumentation, Roll with the Resistance and Support Self-Efficacy. Later versions of MI subsumed the guideline "Avoid Argumentation" into "Roll with the Resistance". In earlier versions of MI, all resistance was regarded as the expression of that side of the ambivalence which was resisting changing the addictive behaviour. In the third edition of Motivational Interviewing (2013), the term "Resistance" was no longer used; instead it was parsed into two constructs: (i) the expression of discord between the client and the interviewer and (ii) the expression of the "don't change" side of ambivalence – now labelled "sustain talk". The psycholinguistic categories of "change talk" and "sustain talk" describe the self-motivating statements in favour of either change or the status quo. Miller and Rollnick (2013) explain that when someone is ambivalent, it is natural to hear change talk and sustain talk intertwined, often within the same sentence reflecting the inner turmoil of simultaneous incentives and disincentives that characterise addiction.

Miller and Rollnick emphasise that in MI the therapist responds selectively to such expressions of ambivalence. Although the key skills in MI are similar to other counselling (e.g. asking open questions, affirming, reflecting and summarising), these skills are practised in a particular fashion in MI. The emphasis is not only on reflecting and summarising the client's feeling but in *selectively reflecting* (emphasis added) or summarising the change talk. According to Miller and Rollnick, summaries tend to reinforce what they contain, whether that is defensiveness, demoralisation, ambivalence or motivation for change. In MI reflective summaries deliberately highlight, emphasise or conclude with the client's own change talk (Miller and Rollnick 2013, page 195).

MI and Problem Gambling

MI is particularly suited for problem gambling because of the high levels of ambivalence, shame and stigma involved in problem gambling. Consequently, MI has been used as a way of preventing dropout during treatment, and it has been included as one component in treatment packages and as a stand-alone treatment. This variety of applications is completely compatible with the original intention of MI – Miller and Rollnick suggested that MI has a synergistic effect when used as preparation for other treatments (Miller and Rollnick 2002; Miller and Rose 2009).

However, this wide variety of contexts, comparisons and definitions can make interpreting the outcome literature difficult. Authors differ in how they define interventions. For example, psychoeducation does not include advice on how to reduce gambling for some authors (Petry 2005), while it does for other authors (Martens et al. 2015). Sometimes brief interventions are compared to MI-CBT treatment packages of longer durations; other times brief MI is compared to CBT without MI components. Sometimes individually delivered MI sessions are compared to other treatments delivered in group format.

Surmounting all these difficulties, in 2015, Yakovenko and colleagues undertook a systematic review of MI in the treatment of disordered (problem, pathological) gambling (Yakovenko et al. 2015). They found a large number (447) of articles describing randomised controlled trials comparing MI to other treatments, of which five with comparable outcome measures were included in a meta-analysis. They concluded that while the reduction in gambling is modest, these results may be meaningful given the low investment of time and resources, especially given the low rates of treatment seeking or completion among problem gamblers. They also support the integration of MI into clinical protocols and self-help tools as is currently done (Ladouceur and Lachance 2007).

MI for Problem Gamblers Seeking Treatment

MI has been shown to reduce dropout from gambling treatment. Even after enrolling in treatment, problem gamblers' motivation to quit fluctuates. Milton et al. (2002) and Wulfert et al. (2003, 2006) successfully used MI strategies to reduce dropout. Milton et al. (2002) randomly assigned problem gamblers to either CBT or CBT plus compliance-enhancing interventions. The compliance-enhancing interventions were a range of strategies, many of which were adapted from MI. These included completing a decisional balance sheet between every appointment, assessment feedback and a therapeutic focus on reinforcing self-efficacy, praise and encouragement for enrolling in therapy and problem solving barriers to change. Milton et al. found that a further 30% of participants completed treatment when given compliance-improving interventions compared to those who received CBT alone.

MI has been included in treatment packages with successful outcomes (Oei et al. 2010; Grant et al. 2009, 2011) It is difficult to evaluate the unique contribution of MI when it is included as one component in a treatment package. Petry et al. 2016 compared a treatment package of four sessions of combined MI and CBT to two very brief (15 min only) interventions (brief advice or psychoeducation). All three groups led to reduced gambling at 5 months, but at 24 months, only the combined MI and CBT group had maintained the improvement. This was despite nearly half of the participants attending only two of the four sessions. Petry et al. note that many gamblers will not attend lengthy treatments. Many gamblers benefit from less intensive treatments, and a stepped care approach to gambling intervention may be warranted (Petry et al. 2016). A comparison of brief, individual MI treatment (four sessions) with eight sessions of group CBT led to a similar conclusion. Both treatments were similar in efficacy, and both treatments were only partially attended (70% of sessions) (Carlbring et al. 2010).

Problems with attendance are even more likely when the participants are not seeking treatment. The majority of problem gamblers do not seek treatment (Petry 2005; Cunningham 2005; Suurvali et al. 2012). Larimer et al. (2011) recruited college students who were either at-risk or probable pathological gamblers but who had not been seeking treatment. They compared one session of MI style personalised feedback with four to six sessions of group CBT. At 6 months both groups had reduced consequences of problem gambling. Only 41% attended half the group sessions even after the number of sessions was reduced to four, whereas 88% attended the single personalised feedback session.

The cost-saving efficiency of MI has surprised some researchers. Toneatto and Gunaratne (2009) randomly allocated problem gamblers to four treatments – cognitive therapy (six sessions), behavioural therapy (six sessions), motivational therapy (six sessions) and a single session of MI. The authors included the single MI session as a control condition for nonspecific natural recovery (page 223). At posttreatment and at 1-year follow-up, all four groups showed similar reductions in gambling frequency and severity. The authors included measures of gambling cognitions such as chasing losses, illusionary control, betting systems, etc. Such thoughts were the explicit focus of the cognitive treatment but not of the other three treatments. Thus, the authors were surprised to find that the single-session MI intervention had the greatest clinical impact on cognitive distortions such as chasing losses. They wrote, "the finding that the single session of MI was able to produce more significant decreases compared to the three longer treatments is difficult to explain satisfactorily" (page 227). According to the authors, it is possible that the provision of a self-help book to the MI group may have given them "an unfair advantage" allowing them to work at their own pace.

The use of MI to enhance self-help materials for problem gamblers was specifically evaluated by Hodgins et al. (2001). Two groups received a CBT self-help workbook in the mail, but half of them underwent MI over the phone lasting between 20 and 45 min before the book was mailed to them. Participants provided the contact details for a collateral to verify their self-report. Both groups were assessed at 1, 3, 6 and 12 months. Those who received the MI phone call had better results at 3 and 6 months but were similar at 12 months, suggesting that the MI had had an effect but that it wore off.

Hodgins and Diskin (2008) provide annotated examples of MI with problem gamblers. This is well worth reading for explicated examples of technique. They cover the main MI strategies, how to summarise, how to explore ambivalence and how to provide normative personalised feedback with permission, how to conduct a decisional balance exercise, and how to encourage self-efficacy. They emphasise that the interviewer needs to use discretion and respond flexibly and sensitively. For example, to insist on a discussion of possible change strategies when the client is not ready or does not believe they have a problem may alienate the client and detract from the purpose of the interview which is to allow clients to access and explore their feelings and thoughts about their gambling. Miller and Rose (2009) have noted that some poor outcomes in manualised MI have occurred when the interviewer has not responded sensitively and flexibly.

Arkowitz et al. (2008) ask, "among the many things yet to be understood with regard to MI is why it has diffused so rapidly" (page 326). They give a number of possible reasons: because so many clients struggle with ambivalence; because of the shift towards evoking motivation rather than trying to install motivation; because it is a relief for clinicians not to have to wrestle; because it helps deal with modest adherence and reduces dropout; and because success can occur with relatively few sessions. Arkowitz et al. (2008) warn that with rapid diffusion comes loose application. Therapists learn the words but not the music. Furthermore, the clinical science of understanding the impact of different components is still at a relatively early stage.

Nonetheless, as this chapter has outlined, brief MI has successfully tapped into a significant need and is compatible with the autonomous desire of many problem gamblers to solve their problem independently (Suurvali et al. 2009) of a complete course of formal treatment.

References

Apodaca, T. R., & Longabaugh, R. (2009). Mechanisms of change in motivational interviewing: A review and preliminary evaluation of the evidence. *Addiction, 104*, 705–715.

Arkowitz, H., Miller, W. R., Westra, H., & Rollnick, S. (2008). Motivational interviewing in the treatment of psychological problems: Conclusions and future directions. In H. Arkowitz, H. A. Westra, W. M. Miller, & S. Rollnick (Eds.), *Motivational interviewing in the treatment of psychological problems*. New York: The Guilford Press.

Carlbring, P., Jonsson, J., Josephson, H., & Forsberg, L. (2010). Motivational interviewing versus cognitive behavioural group therapy in the treatment of problem and pathological gambling: A randomized controlled trial. *Cognitive Behaviour Therapy, 39*(2), 92–103. doi:10.1080/16506070903190245.

Copeland, L., McNamara, R., Kelson, M., & Simpson, S. (2015). Mechanisms of change within motivational interviewing in relation to health behaviors outcomes: A systematic review. *Patient Education and Counseling, 98*, 401–411.

Cunningham, J. A. (2005). Little use of treatment among problem gamblers. *Psychiatric Services, 56*(8), 1024–1025.

Diskin, K. M., & Hodgins, D. C. (2009). A randomised controlled trial of a single session motivational intervention for concerned gamblers. *Behaviour Research and Therapy, 47*, 382–388. doi:10.1016/j.brat.2009.01018.

Grant, J. E., Donahue, C. B., Odlaug, B. L., Kim, S. W., Miller, M. J., & Petry, N. M. (2009). Imaginal desensitisation plus motivational interviewing for pathological gambling: Randomised controlled trial. *British Journal of Psychiatry, 195*, 266–267. doi:10.1192/bjp.bp.108.062414.

Grant, J. E., Donahue, C. B., Odlaug, B. L., & Kim, S. W. (2011). A 6-month follow-up of Imaginal desensitisation plus motivational interviewing in the treatment of pathological gambling. *Annals of Clinical Psychiatry, 23*(1), 3–10.

Hodgins, D. C., Currie, S. R., & el-Guebaly, N. (2001). Motivational enhancement and self-help treatments for problem gambling. *Journal of Consulting and Clinical Psychology, 69*(1), 50–57. doi:1037//0022-006X.69.1.50.

Hodgins, D., & Diskin, K. M. (2008). Motivational interviewing in the treatment of problem and pathological gambling. In H. Arkowitz, H. A. Westra, W. M. Miller, & S. Rollnick (Eds.), *Motivational interviewing in the treatment of psychological problems*. New York: The Guilford Press.

Jones, S. A., Latchford, G., & Tober, G. (2015). Client experiences of motivational interviewing: An interpersonal process recall study. *Psychology and Psychotherapy: Theory, Research and Practice, 89*, 97–114. doi:10.1111/papt.12061.

Ladouceur, R., & Lachance, S. (2007). *Overcoming pathological gambling: Therapist guide*. Oxford: Oxford University Press.

Larimer, M. E., Neighbors, C., Lostutter, T. W., Whiteside, U., Cronce, J. M., Kaysen, D., & Walker, D. (2011). Brief motivational feedback and cognitive behavioral interventions for prevention of disordered gambling: A randomised clinical trial. *Addiction, 107*, 1148–1158. doi:10.1111/j.1360-0443.2011.03776.x.

Martens, M. P., Arterberry, B. J., Takamatsu, S. K., Masters, J., & Dude, K. (2015). The efficacy of a personalized feedback-only intervention for at-risk college gamblers. *Journal of Consulting and Clinical Psychology, 83*(3), 494–499. doi:10.1037/a0038843.

Miller, W. R., & Rollnick, S. (1991). *Motivational interviewing: Preparing people to change addictive behaviour*. New York: The Guilford Press.

Miller, W. R., & Rollnick, S. (2002). *Motivational interviewing: Preparing people for change* (2nd ed.). New York: The Guilford Press.

Miller, W. R., & Rollnick, S. (2013). *Motivational interviewing: Helping people change* (3rd ed.). New York: The Guilford Press.

Miller, W. R., & Rose, G. S. (2009). Toward a theory of motivational interviewing. *American Psychologist, 64*(6), 527–537. doi:10.1037/a0016830.

Milton, S., Crino, R., Hunt, C., & Prosser, E. (2002). The effect of compliance-improving interventions on the cognitive-behavioural treatment of pathological gambling. *Journal of Gambling Studies, 18*(2), 207–229.

Oei, T. P. S., Raylu, N., & Casey, L. M. (2010). Effectiveness of group and individual formats of a combined motivational interviewing and cognitive behavioral treatment program for problem gambling: A randomized controlled trial. *Behavioural and Cognitive Psychotherapy, 38*, 233–238. doi:10.1017/S1352465809990701.

Petry, N. M. (2005). *Pathological gambling: Etiology, comorbidity, and treatment*. Washington: American Psychological Association.

Petry, N. M., Rash, C. J., & Alessi, S. M. (2016). A randomized controlled trial of brief interventions for problem gambling in substance abuse treatment patients. *Journal of Consulting and Clinical Psychology, 84*(10), 874–886. doi:10.1037/ccp0000127.

Suurvali, H., Cordingley, H., Hodgins, D. C., & Cunningham, J. (2009). Barriers to seeking help for gambling problems: A review of the empirical literature. *Journal of Gambling Studies, 25*, 407–424. doi:10.1007/s10899-099-9129-9.

Suurvali, H., Hodgins, D. C., Toneatto, T., & Cunningham, J. A. (2012). Hesitation to seek gambling-related treatment among Ontario problem gamblers. *Journal of Addiction Medicine, 6*(1), 39–49. doi:10.1097/ADM.Ob013e3182307dbb.

Toneatto, T., & Gunaratne, M. (2009). Does treatment of cognitive distortions improve clinical outcomes for problem gambling? *Journal of Contemporary Psychotherapy, 39*, 221–229. doi:10.1007/s10879-009-9119-3.

Westra, H. A., & Dozois, D. J. A. (2008). Integrating motivational into the treatment of anxiety. In H. Arkowitz, H. A. Westra, W. M. Miller, & S. Rollnick (Eds.), *Motivational interviewing in the treatment of psychological problems*. New York: The Guilford Press.

Wulfort, E., Blanchard, E. B., & Martell, R. (2003). Conceptualizing and treating pathological gambling: A motivationally enhanced cognitive behavioral approach. *Cognitive and Behavioral Practice, 10*, 61–72.

Wulfort, E., Blanchard, E., Freidenberg, B. M., & Martell, R. S. (2006). Retaining pathological gamblers in cognitive behaviour therapy through motivational enhancement. A pilot study. *Behavior Modification, 30*(3), 315–340. doi:10.1177/0145445503262578.

Yakovenko, I., Quigley, L., Hemmelgarn, B. R., Hodgins, D. C., & Ronksley, P. (2015). The efficacy of motivational interviewing for disordered gambling: Systematic review and meta-analysis. *Addictive Behaviors, 43*, 72–82. doi:10.1016/j.addbch.201412.011.

Chapter 4
Cognitive Behavioural Therapy for Problem Gambling

Katy O'Neill

It is of course a mistake to assume that once the error in someone's thinking has been pointed out, that is an end to the matter. Helpful responses to automatic thoughts need to be individually tailored, carefully crafted and vividly, imaginatively and frequently rehearsed.

Clients May Not Initially Be Able to Report Their Thoughts

Clients may not be fully aware of the thoughts that occur before they gamble. Habitual smokers or coffee drinkers find themselves pouring another cup or lighting up outside of their conscious awareness. In the same way, the decision to gamble in response to certain triggers may be so well rehearsed that it has become automatic and is below the threshold of awareness (Andrade et al. 2012; Breslin et al. 2002; Kavanagh et al. 2004). When use of a substance is habitual, it is only when such automatic responses are inhibited for some reason (e.g. a decision to abstain or cut down) that the automatic thoughts may intrude into awareness.

Furthermore, gambling is often an attempt to block out awareness of thoughts and worries. Gamblers are often seeking an escape into "the zone" as much as, or at least in addition to, the hope of a win (Schull 2012). It is difficult to provide a detailed account of the thoughts one had during the period one was trying not to be aware of those thoughts.

Finally, many researchers have been struck by the dramatic difference in awareness of gambling thoughts while gambling versus recalling an episode of gambling

K. O'Neill (✉)
St Vincent's Hospital Gambling Treatment Program, St Vincent's Hospital,
390 Victoria St, Darlinghurst, Sydney, NSW 2010, Australia
e-mail: ko@kogo.net.au

C. McIntosh, K. O'Neill, *Evidence-Based Treatments for Problem Gambling*,
SpringerBriefs in Psychology, DOI 10.1007/978-3-319-62485-3_4

(Ladouceur and Walker 1996). Ladouceur and Walker observed that "before and after the game, subjects report that it is a game of chance. Nothing they can do will influence the outcome. During the game, subjects say many things about the game which suggest that the outcome is predictable and can be influenced. It is as if there are two modes of thinking about the game: spontaneous, uncensored reactions to the events in the game while the game is in progress, and rational consideration of the realities of the game when not involved" (page 103).

Increasing Awareness of Automatic Gambling Thoughts

Early in treatment, cognitive therapists educate clients about the cognitive model, explaining that thoughts influence emotions and behaviour. It is vital that clients feel that they will not be judged for the thoughts they report. They may be reluctant to report their thoughts if they don't understand that what is being asked is merely a sample of the stream of ongoing mental chatter they had prior to gambling and they are not being asked about thoughts they endorse after some consideration. Therapists should encourage a non-judgemental approach to the content of clients' thoughts (see the Metacognitive and Mindfulness chapter in this book). Education about how the mind works (e.g. heuristics and illusions) is helpful (see the Psychoeducation chapter of this book).

Toneatto (2002) notes that gambling choices reveal gambling beliefs. He provides a guide for what therapists should listen for when asking about gambling decisions. For example, when asking how the gambler explains wins and losses, listen for attributions of skill when explaining wins and of bad luck or random events when explaining losses. When asking how they decide when to gamble, listen for gut feelings, instinct or intuition.

Often asking the problem gambling client what they think or believe in general terms is less productive than asking them to describe in detail their most recent session of gambling. Ladouceur et al. (2002) describe such an assessment. They suggest keeping an ear out for cognitive distortions but initially refraining from any education which may serve to interrupt the exploration process. The tone is non-judgemental, like the tone used in motivational interviewing (see the Motivational Interviewing chapter in this book).

Ongoing self-monitoring helps clients become more aware of the extent of their gambling in terms of both money and time spent. Monitoring also helps problem gambling clients become more aware of the triggers for gambling thoughts, their responses to gambling thoughts, the duration and intensity of urges and their responses to these. Monitoring also exposes a memory bias of forgetting steady losses. Variations of monitoring forms are provided by most treatment manuals (Blaszczynksi 1998; Ladouceur et al. 2002, Ladouceur and Lachance 2007; Petry 2005; Raylu and Oei 2010.)

Clients' gambling thoughts can be so telescoped or fleeting that they may not even recognise them as present let alone be able to challenge them. They may, for example, hear themselves think "just go" or "forget this" and only on retrospective analysis realise that these thoughts reflect being sick of an internal debate about whether to gamble or not. It is essential therefore to try to catch the exact thought phrase or so-called "hot cognition" rather than thoughts about thoughts.

Labelling the Type of Gambling Thought

Therapists should consider the thoughts that precede a gambling session, occur during a gambling session and follow the gambling session. All three time frames serve to maintain the problem, although it is possible that only those thoughts before and after gambling can be reliably altered through CBT (see below).

Beck et al. (1993) outline three types of addictive beliefs that occur before the decision to use drugs – anticipatory beliefs (positive expectation of some rewarding feeling), relief-oriented beliefs (using will remove an uncomfortable state) and facilitative or permissive beliefs or rationalisations justifying drug use.

In addition to these addictive beliefs, there are gambling-specific superstitions and misunderstandings of probability. Goodie and Fortune (2013) lament that while there is broad agreement that cognitive distortions are involved in pathological gambling, there is no authoritative catalogue of gambling distortions. Toneatto (2002) suggests that ultimately these appear to be related to a core belief or assumption that gambling outcomes can either be influenced (if randomly generated, such as lottery numbers) or predicted (if some, but insufficient, information is available to the gambler, as in horse races or card games). Ejova et al. (2015) conducted a factor analysis and suggest that most erroneous beliefs about gambling fall into two forms of the illusion of control (one a form of gamblers' fallacy, the other a complex set of beliefs about luck and fate).

As noted above, these thoughts don't need to be consistently believed. In the context of an urge to gamble, these thoughts need function only to get the gambler to start gambling. Furthermore, many of these thoughts are believed with conviction only during an urge or during gambling (Sevigny and Ladouceur 2003). Nonetheless, labelling the types of gambling thoughts can help clients step back and see through them. Various authors have provided lists of the types of thoughts that encourage gambling (Griffiths 1994; Ladouceur et al. 2002; Ladouceur and Lachance 2007; Milton 2001; Toneatto 2002; Raylu and Oei 2010).

Tone Is Important When Challenging Gambling Thoughts

Clients may have previously tried to talk themselves out of gambling by internally giving voice to the shame, guilt, remorse and even stupidity that they have felt after losing. This strategy can backfire as it increases the desire to escape, thus intensifying the urge (Kavanagh et al. 2004). Sometimes gambling is an expression of rebellion; certainly it is often advertised as a devil-may-care risk-taking venture. An inner dialogue that is punitive and disapproving only increases the desire to rebel, ironically rebelling against the inner voice that seeks freedom from an addictive slavery.

Self-compassion increases clients' capacity to self-regulate and make difficult changes (Neff 2012; Gilbert 2010). Self-compassion has been linked to reduced rumination, reduced thought suppression, reduced anxiety and reduced depression (Neff 2012). These states of mind have been directly linked to problem gambling (see the Metacognitive and Mindfulness chapter in this book). Gilbert (2010) draws a clear distinction between two approaches to self-correction. One he calls shame-based self-attacking and the other he calls compassionate self-correction. Shame-based self-attacking focuses on the desire to condemn and punish and is given with anger, frustration and contempt. Shame-based self-attacking focuses on a global sense of self, lowers mood and increases the chances of avoidance and escape into destructive behaviours. In contrast, compassionate self-correction focuses on the desire to improve, is given with encouragement and support and increases the chances of engaging in constructive behaviours. Clients are often reluctant to adopt a self-compassionate tone with themselves. They seem to believe that abusive yelling at themselves is not only deserving; it will be effective – even if it has not worked thus far. This view of how to change can perpetuate problem gambling and needs to be addressed. Adding self-loathing when one is dealing with an urge does not energise one to ride out the urge.

Sometimes the desire to go gambling has become a proxy for a legitimate goal which has been hijacked by a gambling habit. Clients may have genuine reasons for not wanting to go home after work; they may have fantasies of reparation ("one last win and I'll pay everyone back and then I'll stop"); they may be lonely and want the apparent company of a venue; they may wish to escape their worries, memories or grief; or they may be bored. The consequence of gambling in response to stress is that eventually all sorts of triggers become linked to a desire to escape through gambling. That is, the triggers generalise, and everything becomes a reason to gamble. Some gamblers like solving puzzles and don't like to give up. In almost any other context, say, the pursuit of knowledge rather than gambling, such persistence would be admirable even if quixotic. Acknowledging the possibility that legitimate unmet needs underlie some gambling urges helps the client frame their inner dialogue in a self-compassionate way and come up with constructive alternatives.

Delfabbro (2004) has excellent advice on how to present counter arguments to gamblers. In an article titled "The Stubborn Logic of Regular Gamblers" he suggests that insisting on challenging gamblers' beliefs can make them feel resentful or foolish. Rather one could acknowledge that they are not necessarily more irrational than anyone else in society, but they are applying heuristics in an inappropriate environment.

By modelling compassionate curiosity during the session rather than impatience or incredulity, the therapist is a model for how the client is to respond to their own thoughts.

Challenges to Urge Thoughts Require a Higher Standard of Evidence than Urge Thoughts

Urge thoughts need only get the client to start gambling. They are overlearned, occur automatically, offer the hope of a win and, regardless of a win, promise excitement and escape. In contrast, the thoughts that keep a client from gambling may be prosaic, do not promise immediate gratification, offer no chance of an immediate win and may not spring to mind convincingly when needed.

The responses to gambling thoughts therefore need to be prepared, well-rehearsed, linked to personally meaningful goals, and vividly memorable to be available for the client to bring them to mind during an urge. Gambling thoughts often have a veneer of reason – e.g. "it's my money" or "I've won before". To argue with the literal content of these thoughts during an urge is to miss the point – which is why such thoughts are such effective facilitating thoughts. During the internal urge debate, the client needs to have already prepared arguments for not gambling that are constructive, self-compassionate, emotional and personally relevant (Harris et al. 2016). They would also benefit from including some short-term advantage to not gambling such as avoiding an argument (Kavanagh et al. 2004). These counter thoughts also need to be hard to discount or ignore, hence accurate. Responses such as "I never win" or "I won't win" don't work because they fly in the face of what the gambler has experienced and logic as it is the nature of gambling that one does not know when the next win might occur.

Gamblers often have a temporal amnesia about their gambling expenditure. When caught up in an urge, they frequently reset their expenditure clock to zero while vividly remembering previous wins. This perpetual resetting of the balance sheet makes gambling more appealing by taking it out of its true financial context. One response to this is for gamblers to remind themselves of the running cumulative tally of expenditure versus wins, perhaps by keeping a card with the ratio written on it in their wallet, purse or mobile phone (Allcock 1994 cited in Ladouceur and Walker 1996).

Making Probabilities More Vivid

This recommendation was made by the Australian Productivity Commission (1999). In a section titled "Communicating the Price of Gambling", they suggested that more evocative ways of representing odds could be used. For example, based on the manufacturers' specifications of a then popular game, to have just a 50% chance of the jackpot, it would take 6.7 million button presses or 392 days of continuous play (24 h per day) or cost nearly $33,000. Another way of communicating the cost might be the cost per hour of various bet choices although this may vary too much to be meaningful – e.g. the Responsible Gambling Guide (2013) from the Victorian Responsible Gambling Foundation notes that for a one dollar per single line bet you can expect to lose over $218 per hour. The concept of an amount of money is familiar and vivid; we can think of what could be purchased such as clothing, a car, a holiday, etc. The concept of odds however is less intuitive and less familiar. The Australian Gaming Machine Manufacturers Association publishes a Player Information Booklet (Australian Gaming Machine Manufacturers Association, undated). This booklet provides the example that the chance of the top prize in some gaming machines is 1 in 9,765,625. This fact can be easily passed over. However, if a gambler is slowly taken through an imaginary exercise of imagining everyone in Sydney, "Have you been to Sydney, imagine everyone in Richmond, Penrith, Bondi (suburbs of Sydney), can you picture all those people? Now imagine everyone in Melbourne, everyone in Brunswick, everyone on Collins Street… Now imagine everyone in Canberra… Now imagine a birds' eye view of all those people and now choose just one of those people". This gives a better sense of the odds of 1 in 9 million.

Thoughts After a Gambling Session Can Maintain the Problem

To an outsider, one of the more striking things about problem gambling is how persistently hope triumphs over experience. It seems akin to the panic sufferer who despite having survived hundreds if not thousands of panic attacks, still believes that the next panic attack could be the one that kills them. In the case of panic, subtle safety behaviours lead the sufferer to conclude that they would have died if not for the safety behaviour, so each panic is interpreted as a "close shave" rather than evidence of the inherent harmlessness of panic. In the case of gambling, some types of thoughts serve a similar maintaining function.

Biased evaluations of outcome: A double standard of attributions for wins and losses maintains whatever illusions of skill or influence that the gambler has (Toneatto 2002; Ladouceur and Walker 1996). Wins are attributed to skill, that is, confirmation of successful prediction or influence, while losses are attributed to bad luck or randomness, that is, discounted or explained way.

Next time I will quit while I am ahead: After losing more than intended, a gambler can look back over a session and see a moment when they would have broken even, or at least not lost so much, if only they had left before they finally did. So rather than learning a lesson of near inevitable loss, they tell themselves that next time they will leave earlier. Most EGM gamblers will have had the experience of either leaving after a big win or at least leaving with a goodly portion of that win, so it seems plausible that they can do so again. Such rare events are unfortunately etched more vividly into memory than the many more times they left with nothing. Large wins impact the SEEKING pathway (Panksepp 1998) differently than do a series of smaller wins. Large wins provide a form of "stop signal" that smaller nibbles or teasers do not. (The SEEKING pathway is discussed in the Psychoeducation chapter of this book.) Information about the SEEKING pathway and recognising that the timing of any large win is determined by algorithm and also reviewing their own history of being "stuck at a machine" helps problem gamblers come to realise that their capacity to leave is in fact largely determined by chance and not by their own determination or intention. It is natural and normal to lose control over play during session on an EMG (Dickerson and O'Connor 2006). In fact, the machines are designed to maximise the players "time on device (TOD)" (Schull 2012).

"It's only money" and other potentially life-saving maladaptive rationalisations: Sometimes after heavy losses, gamblers remind themselves that it's only money. This type of thinking may prevent them from being overwhelmed with guilt, shame and remorse and might even be an alternative to suicidal thoughts. Pathological gamblers have much higher rates of suicidal thinking, attempted suicide and suicide than the general population (Maccallum and Blaszczynski 2003). But such amelioration of the emotional consequences of gambling can of course contribute to ongoing gambling. Parke et al. (2007) described a wide range of maladaptive positive thinking after losses on slot machines (EGMs). They noted that misguided positive thinking disrupted naturally occurring contingencies that might otherwise prevent excessive gambling (Parke et al. page 51). Similarly, Navas et al. (2016) found that the use of some emotion regulation strategies such as "refocusing on planning" and "putting into perspective" which are generally adaptive in other contexts predicted the severity of gambling problems.

Resolutions: "I feel so bad I know I'll never go gambling again". Sometimes the losses lead to an epiphany "I'll never gamble again!" And for a period, this may be true. When clients enter treatment, their losses are usually more recent than their wins (Toneatto 2002). Such epiphanies and their repeated subsequent abandonment make for harrowing reading in Fyodor Dostoyevsky's *The Gambler* (Dostoyevsky 1966). The author (KO) quizzed many gamblers who expressed such epiphanies to ascertain if there was a way to distinguish between those expressions which did lead to abstinence and those which did not. Eventually what became clear was that there was no difference in the content of these expressions but rather in what subsequent constructive actions the problem gambler took to protect the epiphany.

The Use of Imagery to Inhibit the Elaboration of Desires

According to Elaborated Intrusion Theory (Kavanagh et al. 2005), there are two components to an episode of craving: an initial apparently spontaneous intrusive thought followed by a cycle of elaborated cognition. The thought feels spontaneous, because we have been unaware of the precursor activity, which takes the form of automatic or overlearned associations that do not require conscious control (Andrade et al. 2012). In some problem gamblers, the absence of any money provides a relief from craving as they feel unable to convincingly elaborate on the initial intrusion.

Anyone attempting to abstain in the presence of such an intrusive desire is faced with a seemingly impossible dilemma. Attempts to suppress such thoughts will usually backfire. Suppression is believed to backfire as it involves monitoring for the thought which increases its salience and availability (Kavanagh et al. 2004). Elaborative processing on the other hand maintains the intrusion. The elaborated intrusion exacerbates the desire, which in turn increases a sense of lack. In someone attempting to abstain, this sense of lack may lead to pessimism or guilt and other negative emotions which have previously been associated with substance use (Kavanagh et al. 2004). A vicious circle indeed!

If neither suppression nor elaboration is fruitful, what strategy can be adopted in response to an intrusive desire? One approach is mindfulness (see the Metacognitive and Mindfulness chapter in this book). Andrade et al. (2012) found that mentally scanning the body works to reduce cravings by shifting attention towards increased awareness of experiences and thoughts other than the unwanted ones (page 19). Interestingly, body scanning is often one of the components of mindfulness training (see the Metacognitive and Mindfulness chapter in this book).

Another approach is proposed by Kavanagh and his colleagues. They cite research showing that attention diversion shows promise. They have shown that sensory (visual, olfactory, aural, tactile, etc.) imagery is a key conscious process in this elaborative processing and that it makes demands on limited attentional and memory resources. They suggest this competition of desires and other tasks for limited working memory resources offers intriguing possibilities for intervention. They have been able to show that effortful visual processing (e.g. forming complex visual imagery such as a tennis game) diminishes craving (Kavanagh et al. 2005). Although this approach has been applied successfully to a range of addictions and to food cravings in dieters, it has not yet been applied specifically to gambling urges. Harvey et al. (2004) noting that thought suppression leads to further intrusions explain how distraction can work to reduce intrusions. They outline behavioural experiments with clients, first showing through the well-known white bear experiment (don't think of a white bear – can I not think of a white bear? – oops I just did!), that thought suppression leads to further intrusions. Secondly showing that if one turns one's attention to a new positive distractor unrelated to the intrusive thoughts, one can learn that one's thoughts are not out of control. Harvey et al. note that ironic process theory suggests that it is better to try and think of a positive thought (an approach goal) than to try and not think of a negative thought (an avoidance goal) (Harvey et al. (2004, page 233)). In this case, distraction becomes a wise metacognitive allocation of attention!

Stott et al. (2010) have another reason to suggest the active generation of alternative visual images or scripts. When clients repeatedly focus on one recurrent script, they forget that other alternatives scripts are as plausible as the one they are ruminating on. Similarly, Longmore and Worrell (2007) argue that therapy should also construct and strengthen helpful representations, rather than just limiting itself to the logico-deductive or rational challenging of unhelpful representations. The act of generating such alternatives allows the client to be more sceptical of their usual ruminative script. This scepticism of the content of one's mind is a process of stepping back from the content of one's thoughts – another component of mindful detachment (see the Metacognitive and Mindfulness chapter in this book).

Use of Guided Imagery in Rehearsal: Imaginal Desensitisation

One particular example of rehearsing guided imagery is imaginal desensitisation. Rather than only intellectualising a reason not to go gambling during the therapy session, the client learns to create and recreate a visceral experience, a rehearsal of an alternative script.

Imaginal desensitisation involves the client imagining a series of prepared scenes while remaining relaxed. One scene creates an urge, and then later scenes have them remembering the aversive consequences and imagining themselves losing interest in gambling and walking away and feeling good. The relaxation is incompatible with the urge to complete the imagined gambling. Imaginal desensitisation has been shown to work with problem gamblers (McConaghy et al. 1991; Dowling et al. 2007; Grant et al. 2009). It has also been effective as home practice (Blaszczynski et al. 2005) and is described in a self-help book (Blaszczynksi 1998). Imaginal desensitisation has several likely effective components. Apart from the original theoretical aim of reducing the arousal associated with urges, it also involves repeatedly mentally associating the urge to gamble with the negative consequences and repeatedly rehearsing an effective response in imagination as well as associating refraining from gambling with feeling good and at ease.

Unanswered Questions About CBT for Problem Gambling

Cognitive distortions are not unique to problem gamblers. Non-gamblers show the same distortions and illusions as gamblers (Petry 2005) although at lower rates (Griffiths 1994; Cunningham et al. 2014) or with less conviction (Ladouceur 2004). Petry (2005) notes that these illusions and distortions are present in all aspects of life that involve making decisions that have uncertain outcomes. Research to date is inconsistent about the direct relationship between these cognitive distortions and the severity of gambling. Some research has found gamblers express reasonable knowledge of mathematical reasoning ability when not actually playing (Lambos and Delfabbro 2007). Other research has found mathematical reasoning is lacking in gamblers even when not playing (Cunningham et al. 2014). Ladouceur and Walker (1996) conclude that cognitive distortions by themselves cannot be regarded as a complete explanation of why people gamble to excess.

Does CBT change problem gamblers' cognitive distortions? Petry (2005) notes that research has not yet demonstrated whether cognitive therapy that focuses on irrational cognitions actually does modify them. Other authors have acknowledged the difficulty of profoundly shifting some distorted gambling cognitions (Delfabbro 2004; Toneatto 2012). Some have questioned whether challenging gambling-related cognitions is the only way to reduce gambling or even gambling-related cognitions (Toneatto and Gunaratne 2009). Even if a gambler's cognitions change outside play, it is uncertain that they change during play. "Faulty cognitions appear inherent in gambling situations" (Petry 2005, page 212). This is not surprising if we allow that as in evolutionary mismatch theory (Spinella 2003), some gambling distortions are human heuristics elicited and heightened by the act of gambling (see the "Psychoeducation" chapter in this book).

Conclusion

Cognitive distortions are unquestionably at play in problem gambling, and CBT does show some benefit. Rather than focusing exclusively on changing these beliefs or preventing them from ever arising, being able to deal constructively with the ebb and flow of such thoughts may be how problem gamblers cease gambling. This is how a metacognitive stance and mindful detachment are relevant. (See the "Metacognitive and Mindfulness Approaches" chapter in this book.)

References

Andrade, J., May, J., & Kavanagh, D. (2012). Sensory imagery in craving: from cognitive psychology to new treatments for addiction. *Journal of Experimental Psychopathy, 3*(2), 127–145. doi:10.5127/jep.024611.

Australian Gaming Machine Manufacturers Association. (undated). Player Information Booklet.

Beck, A. T., Wright, F. D., Newman, C. F., & Liese, B. S. (1993). *Cognitive therapy of substance abuse*. New York: The Guilford Press.

Blaszczynksi, A. (1998). *Overcoming compulsive gambling: A self-help guide using cognitive behavioural techniques*. London: Robinson.

Blaszczynski, A., Drobny, J., & Steel, Z. (2005). Home-based imaginal desensitisation in pathological gambling: Short-term outcomes. *Behaviour Change, 22*(1), 13–21.

Breslin, F. C., Zack, M., & McMain, S. (2002). An information-processing analysis of mindfulness: Implications for relapse prevention in the treatment of substance abuse. *Clinical Psychology: Science and Practice, 9*(3), 275–299.

Cunningham, J. A., Hodgins, D. C., & Toneatto, T. (2014). Relating severity of gambling to cognitive distortions in a representative sample of problem gamblers. *Journal of Gambling Issues, 29*, 1–16. doi:10.4309/jgi.2014.29.2.

Delfabbro, P. (2004). The stubborn logic of regular gamblers: Obstacles and dilemmas in cognitive gambling research. *Journal of Gambling Studies, 20*(1), 1–21.

Dickerson, M., & O'Connor, J. (2006). *Gambling as an addictive behaviour: Impaired control, harm minimisation, treatment and prevention*. Cambridge: Cambridge University Press.

Dostoyevsky, F. (1966). *The Gambler*. Penguin Books edition 1966. London: Penguin Books.

Dowling, N., Smith, D., & Thomas, T. (2007). A comparison of individual and group cognitive-behavioural treatment for female pathological gambling. *Behaviour Research and Therapy, 45*, 2192–2202. doi:1016/j.brat.2006.11.003.

Ejova, A., Delfabbro, P., & Navarro, D. J. (2015). Erroneous gambling-related beliefs as illusions of primary and secondary control: A confirmatory factor analysis. *Journal of Gambling Studies, 31*, 133–160. doi:10.1007/s10899-013-9402-9.

Gilbert, P. (2010). *Compassion focused therapy: Distinctive features*. London: Routledge.

Goodie, A. S., & Fortune, E. E. (2013). Measuring cognitive distortions in pathological gambling: Review and meta-analysis. *Psychology of Addictive Behaviors, 27*(3), 730–743. doi: 101037/a0031892.

Grant, J. E., Donahue, C. B., Odlaug, B. L., Kim, S. W., Miller, M. J., & Petry, N. M. (2009). Imaginal desensitisation plus motivational interviewing for pathological gambling: Randomised controlled trial. *The British Journal of Psychiatry, 195*, 266–267. doi:10.1192/bjp.bp.108.062414.

Griffiths, M. D. (1994). The role of cognitive bias and skill in fruit machine gambling. *British Journal of Psychology, 85*, 351–369.

Harris, A., Parke, A., & Griffiths, M. D. (2016). The case for using personally relevant and emotionally stimulating gambling messages as a gambling harm-minimisation strategy. *International Journal of Mental Health and Addiction.* doi:10.1007/s11469-016-9698-7.

Harvey, A. G., Watkins, E., Mansell, W., & Shafran, R. (2004). *Cognitive behavioural processes across psychological disorders: A transdiagnostic approach to research and treatment*. Oxford: Oxford University Press.

Kavanagh, D. J., Andrade, J., & May, J. (2004). Beating the urge: Implications of research into substance-related desires. *Addictive Behaviors, 29*, 1359–1372. doi:10.1016/j.addbeh.2004.06.009.

Kavanagh, D. J., Andrade, J., & May, J. (2005). Imaginary relish and exquisite torture: The elaborated intrusion theory of desire. *Psychological Review, 112*(2), 446–467. doi:10.1037/0033-295X.112.2.446.

Ladouceur, R. (2004). Perceptions among pathological and nonpathological gamblers. *Addictive Behaviors, 29*, 555–565. doi:10.1016/j.addbeh.2003.08.025.

Ladouceur, R., & Lachance, S. (2007). *Overcoming pathological gambling: Therapist guide*. Oxford: Oxford University Press.

Ladouceur, R., & Walker, M. (1996). A cognitive perspective on gambling. In P. M. Salkovskis (Ed.), *Trends in cognitive and behavioral therapies*. Chichester: John Wiley and Sons.

Ladouceur, R., Sylvain, C., Boutin, C., & Doucet, C. (2002). *Understanding and treating the pathological gambler*. Chichester: John Wiley and Sons.

Lambos, C., & Delfabbro, P. (2007). Numerical reasoning ability and irrational beliefs in problem gambling. *International Gambling Studies, 7*(2), 157–171. doi:10.1080/14459790701387428.

Longmore, R. J., & Worrell, M. (2007). Do we need to challenge thoughts in cognitive behaviour therapy? *Clinical Psychology Review, 27*, 173–187. doi:10.1016/j.cpr.2006.08.001.

Maccallum, F., & Blaszczynski, A. (2003). Pathological gambling and suicidality: An analysis of severity and lethality. *Suicide and Life-threatening Behavior, 33*(1), 88–98.

McConaghy, N., Blaszczynski, A., & Frankova, A. (1991). Comparison of imaginal desensitisation with other behavioural treatments of pathological gambling: a two to nine year follow-up. *British Journal of Psychiatry, 159*, 390–393.

Milton, S. (2001). *Stop gambling: A self-help manual for giving up gambling*. Sydney: Pan Macmillan.

Navas, J. F., Verdejo-Garcia, A., Lopez-Gomez, M., Maldonado, A., & Perales, J. C. (2016). Gambling with rose-tinted glasses on: Use of emotion-regulation strategies correlates with dysfunctional cognitions in gambling disorder patients. *Journal of Behavioral Addictions, 5*(2), 271–281. doi:10.1556/2006.5.2016.040.

Neff, K. D. (2012). The science of self-compassion. In C. K. Germer & R. D. Siegel (Eds.), *Wisdom and compassion in psychotherapy*. New York: Guilford Press.

Panksepp, J. (1998). *Affective neuroscience: The foundations of human and animal emotions*. Oxford: Oxford University Press.

Parke, J., Griffiths, M. D., & Parke, A. (2007). Positive thinking among slot machine gamblers: A case of maladaptive coping? *International Journal Mental and Addiction, 5*, 39–52. doi:10.1007/s11469-006-9049-1.

Petry, N. M. (2005). *Pathological gambling: etiology, comorbidity, and treatment*. Washington: American Psychological Association.

Productivity Commission. (1999). *Australia's gambling industries*, Summary, Report No. 10, AusIndo Canberra.

Raylu, N., & Oei, T. P. (2010). *A cognitive behavioural therapy programme for problem gambling: Therapist manual*. London: Routledge.

Schull, N. D. (2012). *Addiction by design: Machine gambling in Las Vegas*. Princeton NJ: Princeton University Press.
Sevigny, S., & Ladouceur, R. (2003). Gamblers' irrational thinking about chance events: The 'double switching concept. *International Gambling Studies, 3*(2), 163–170.
Spinella, M. (2003). Evolutionary mismatch, neural reward circuits, and pathological gambling. *International Journal of Neuroscience, 113*, 503–512. doi:10.1080/00207450390162254.
Stott, R., Mansell, W., Salkovskis, P., Lavender, A., & Cartwright-Hatton, S. (2010). *Oxford Guide to Metaphors in CBT* (p. 2010). Oxford: Oxford University Press.
Toneatto, T. (2002). Cognitive therapy for problem gambling. *Cognitive and behavioural practice, 9*, 191–199.
Toneatto, T. (2012). Mindfulness-based therapy for problem gambling. In S. C. Hayes & M. E. Levin (Eds.), *Mindfulness and acceptance for addictive behaviors*. Oakland CA: New Harbinger Publications.
Toneatto, T., & Gunaratne, M. (2009). Does treatment of cognitive distortions improve clinical outcomes for problem gambling? *Journal of Contemporary Psychotherapy, 39*, 221–229. doi:10.1007/s10879-009-9119-3.
Victorian Responsible Gambling Foundation. (2013). *The responsible gambling guide*. State Government Victoria.

Chapter 5
Metacognitive and Mindfulness Approaches to Problem Gambling

Katy O'Neill

Metacognitive Therapy

It can sometimes be difficult to categorise particular thoughts or beliefs as metacognitive or not. This difficulty is apparent through the literature. Metacognitions are implicit in "traditional" cognitive behaviour therapy (CBT) (Harvey et al. 2004; Stott et al. 2010). Nonetheless the "science of CBT" is moving towards an explicit focus on metacognition rather than it being merely implied (Dobson 2013). Metacognitive treatments largely target maladaptive responses to thoughts, that is, reactions to reactions (Williams 2010), such as attempts to suppress or to elaborate. Metacognitive treatments target how the thoughts are processed and function rather than the actual content of the thoughts. These treatments all argue that what maintains or exacerbates distress is the response to inner experience, such as an urge, rather than the initial occurrence of the urge. To paraphrase Martin Luther, "You cannot keep birds from flying over your head, but you can keep them from building a nest in your hair".

The content of thoughts may change, even as the function of the thought remains. For example, after discussing how some features of electronic gaming machines (EGMs) entice the player, more than one client has had thoughts such as, "I should go and play to see if what my therapist described actually does happen". The content of this thought is novel, but the function (to motivate or justify playing) is not. If one were to respond only to the content, one would be reinventing the wheel over and over.

K. O'Neill (✉)
St Vincent's Hospital Gambling Treatment Program, St Vincent's Hospital,
390 Victoria St, Darlinghurst, Sydney, NSW 2010, Australia
e-mail: ko@kogo.net.au

C. McIntosh, K. O'Neill, *Evidence-Based Treatments for Problem Gambling*,
SpringerBriefs in Psychology, DOI 10.1007/978-3-319-62485-3_5

Problem Gamblers Show Metacognitive Deficits

Individuals with problem gambling have been shown to have some impaired metacognitive capacities, namely, an impaired ability to assess their own abilities during gambling (Brevers et al. 2013) and during non-gambling tasks (Brevers et al. 2014). The authors suggest that problem gambling is associated with poor insight as a general factor and that this poor insight maintains problem gambling as the individual is less able to learn from experience. While an impaired capacity may have predisposed individuals to gambling, a plausible alternative possibility is that impaired capacity results from many years practising a behaviour where skill is only slightly if at all correlated with outcome.

Metacognitions in Problem Gambling

When clinicians focus on metacognitions, they are usually referring to a subset of metacognitive factors that maintain psychological distress. These include evaluative metacognitions that stress discomfort or prescriptive metacognitions that construe the cognitive state as one which must be modified. Such metacognitions leave individuals susceptible to substance abuse (Toneatto 1995 page 96). Maladaptive metacognitions about avoiding inner experience can drive problem gambling in anxious and depressed problem gamblers (Lindberg et al. 2011; Jauregu et al. 2016; Mansueto et al. 2016). These authors suggest that given the well-documented levels of comorbidity in problem gamblers, treatment should include assessment of the metacognitions associated with maladaptive coping of anxiety and depression. These authors used the Metacognitions Questionnaire 30 MCQ-30 (Wells and Cartwright-Hatton 2004) to do so, but they did not assess metacognitions about gambling.

It is, however, important to assess metacognitions specifically about gambling. Firstly, not all problem gambling is necessarily an attempt to escape. The pathways model proposes that not all gamblers are emotionally vulnerable (Blaszczynski and Nowrer 2002). Secondly, it is only when gambling cognitions or metacognitions themselves are assessed that their role can be revealed. Raylu et al. (2016) found that avoidance coping predicted gambling behaviour only indirectly via gambling cognitions. They used the gambling expectancies subscale of the GRCS (Gambling-Related Cognitions Scale) (Raylu and Oei 2004). The GRCS includes metacognitions about using gambling to regulate emotions (e.g. "gambling makes me happier", "gambling helps reduce tension and stress"). Similarly, Fernie et al. (2014) found that metacognitions about gambling predicted gambling behaviour.

Metacognitive Theories of Addiction

A number of researchers have put forward metacognitive theories of addiction. In 1995 Toneatto proposed a metacognitive model of substance use – the Regulation of Cognitive States (RCS) model. He suggested substances or gambling can quickly and effectively modify unpleasant affective states or cognitive events, primarily through the reduction of awareness. Thus, they provide relief, sometimes described as feeling numb or escaping aversive self-awareness. Toneatto (1999b) emphasises two types of metacognitions: (i) beliefs about the effects of use such as relief from anxiety, anger, stress and reduced self-awareness of negative thoughts, in other words, negatively reinforced escape and (ii) beliefs about the consequences of not using, such as dreading the discomfort that would result or fearing that the negative internal state would intensify and persist.

Kavanagh and colleagues proposed the elaborated intrusion (EI) theory of desire. They noted that desires (e.g. to use drugs, to gamble) involve both associative and elaborative processes. Substance use becomes associated with a wide range of cues – some internal (e.g. emotional distress) and some external (e.g. time of day, presence of money). Associative processes, triggered by both environmental and internal cues, initiate episodes of desire (Kavanagh et al. 2004). The two typical responses to such intrusions, namely, elaboration or attempts at suppression both exacerbate the problem (see "Cognitive Behaviour Therapy" chapter in this book). Interestingly, independent researchers initially working in the area of generalised anxiety disorder also describe two opposing maladaptive metacognitive control strategies that play a role in maintaining the distress of worry. Wells (2000) described positive beliefs about worry (that it helps solve problems, etc.) and negative beliefs (e.g. that worry is uncontrollable). Well's metacognitive therapy model has been adapted to substance abuse and gambling (Spada et al. 2014, 2015). Positive metacognitive beliefs motivate continued thinking and attention such as "if I think about gambling I may come up with a winning system" or "gambling helps me forget about my problems". Negative metacognitive beliefs concern the significance, uncontrollability or danger of thoughts such as "having an urge to gamble means deep down I want to destroy myself and my family". Kavanagh et al. (2004) note that one of the most distressing aspects of urges is concern over their meaning (reframing the meaning of urges is discussed in "Psychoeducation" chapter of this book).

Assessing for Relevant Metacognitions in Addiction Treatment

Toneatto (1995, 1999a) suggests that clinicians assess what cognitive/affective states clients have difficulty coping with and that they use alcohol, drugs or gambling to modify (e.g. boredom, fatigue, anger, sadness). The clinicians ask about expectancies, that is, beliefs about the effects of drinking, using drugs or gambling on that particular cognitive state. For example, what effect do they expect gambling would have on their boredom or worry? Clients might describe direct relief or at least a reduction in self-awareness of the distress (e.g. gambling to forget worries). Toneatto labels these “metacognitive effect” beliefs. Clinicians should also assess what clients believe would happen if they were unable to modify a cognitive state by drinking or gambling. Responses might include fear that the boredom would go on and on, that it would get worse and that they would not be able to cope or sleep due to inescapable worry. He labels these “metacognitive consequences”. Making both the metacognitive consequences and the metacognitive effects explicit provides crucial clinical information about what beliefs mediate between inner experience and the decision to drink, use drugs or gamble to ameliorate it.

Similarly, Spada et al. (2012) suggest conducting an AMC analysis (A is the activating thought, M is the metacognitive plan and C are the affective consequences). The activating thought is followed by the metacognitive plan which consists of the individual’s metacognitive beliefs (e.g. that the feeling must be controlled) and procedural blueprints that guide coping (e.g. that drinking will help reduce the feeling). This is followed by the affective consequences (drinking and a reduction in the feeling). Spada et al. (2014) provide an interview template for profiling the metacognitive beliefs in problem gambling. The gambling expectancies subscale of the GRCS (Gambling-Related Cognitions Scale) (Raylu and Oei 2004) dovetails neatly into an assessment of metacognitive beliefs about gambling.

The reader may notice that many of the beliefs labelled as metacognitive are familiar to researchers and clinicians applying traditional cognitive behaviour therapy. This is certainly true. Nonetheless, explicitly noting the role these thoughts have in perpetuating the problem is an important addition to challenging their content.

Taking a Metacognitive Stance

Taking a metacognitive stance involves taking a fundamentally different view of one’s own inner experiences. Harvey et al. (2004) note that “decentring” or “metacognitive awareness” is an important aspect of metacognitive regulation. Decentring is defined as the ability to view thoughts as mental events in a wider context of awareness rather than as expressions of reality. It is the ability to step back from thoughts and see them as ideas to be tested rather than facts (Harvey et al. 2004). Toneatto et al. (2007) suggest that, “learning to relate differently to gambling cognitions may be as important as, if not more important than, challenging the specific contents of the thoughts” (page 94).

One component of metacognitive treatment involves modifying metacognitive beliefs directly (Spada et al. 2012; Harvey et al. 2004). Beliefs about the nature of urges and what they mean can be challenged directly (see “Psychoeducation” chapter in this book). Spada et al. (2012) suggest strategies for tackling such metacognitive beliefs include traditional cognitive techniques. For example, careful history taking can reveal that in the past, clients will have had urges that they could not satisfy yet faded over time.

Another component of metacognitive treatment could be guided exposure to avoided cognitive states (Toneatto 1995). Analogous to exposure to phobic objects to reduce avoidance, the exposure would ideally provide the client with disconfirmation of dysfunctional beliefs such as "I just cannot stand boredom at all", "if I don't drink when I'm bored I'll go crazy", etc. The aim of such exposure is for clients to learn that while cognitive and affective events are very real subjectively, they are also temporary, difficult to control and inherently harmless.

An alternative to such guided exposure is mindfulness. As discussed in the "Psychoeducation" and "Cognitive Behaviour Therapy" chapters in this book, some gambling thoughts occur with associated physiological arousal. These intrusions are experienced as more than a mildly interesting possibility but with feelings of excitement and hope. Mindfulness training allows clients to practise the skill of stepping back from such inner experiences.

Mindfulness-Based Interventions for Problem Gambling

Kabat-Zinn (2013) notes that there has been an "avalanche" of interest in mindfulness in clinical research, from a trickle of papers in the late 1990s to hundreds per year in the 2000s. For a review see Creswell (2017). Various mindfulness-based interventions or interventions that include mindfulness as a component (e.g. acceptance and commitment therapy (ACT), dialectical behaviour therapy (DBT), mindfulness-based stress reduction (MBSR), mindfulness-based cognitive therapy (MBCT)) have been shown to be effective in treating the disorders that are often comorbid with gambling. Of more direct relevance to problem gambling, mindfulness-based interventions have been shown to be effective in substance use disorders. For reviews see Zgierska et al. (2009) and Chiesa and Serretti (2014). Mindfulness-based relapse prevention (MBRP) (Witkiewitz et al. 2005) is discussed in the Relapse Prevention chapter of this book.

What Is Mindfulness Training?

Mindfulness and meditation, although often confused, are not the same thing. Theoretically, a person can be mindful during any activity. Mindfulness training is a type of meditation in which one formally practises mindfulness while meditating. Breslin et al. (2002) contrast mindfulness meditation with relaxation meditation. In relaxation meditation, the individual focuses attention on an object (e.g. the breath, a candle, a repeated mantra, or a guided meditation) and attempts to ignore distracting mental events. In contrast, in mindfulness meditation, the individual has a different attitude to distracting thoughts. One observes them with curiosity and tolerance rather than elaborating or suppressing them. In this way one learns to change how one relates to dysfunctional thoughts and negative affect rather than attempting to eliminate them.

Mindfulness meditation is not about clearing the mind. Nor is it a way of blissing out or about getting rid of natural processes such as thinking. Rather, meditation is about coming to see where natural, automatic reactions stop and elaboration or avoidance processes begin. During mindfulness meditation, we pay attention to our reactions, particularly reactions of wanting positive states to last, negative states to end and neutral states to be less boring (Williams 2010). The word "acceptance" is often used. This is not passive resignation but rather a willingness to experience the mental event without rumination, elaboration, suppression or avoidance.

Why Do Mindfulness Training? Possible Benefits for Problem Gamblers

Many authors have enumerated the putative mechanisms of mindfulness training. What follows is a partial list of those that may be relevant to problem gambling. It has long been acknowledged that much of our day-to-day behaviour is mindless, that we live with an "unbearable automaticity of being" (Bargh and Chartrand 1999). Breslin et al. (2002) suggest that one benefit of mindfulness training would be an "increased awareness of overlearned patterns of thoughts and emotions". Mindfulness training has been shown to reduce mindless, automatic responding to mental events through improving executive functions (Alfonso et al. 2011). Both are highly relevant to the overlearned behaviour of problem gambling.

Another benefit is that mindfulness reduces rumination and thought suppression (Creswell 2017). As noted above, rumination and thought suppression are metacognitive factors that exacerbate anxiety and stress, both highly comorbid with problem gambling. In a similar vein, Andrade et al. (2012) suggest that training in mindfulness would break the cycle of attempted thought suppression or elaboration of craving intrusions. Mindfulness modifies the relationship to mental events (Daubenmier et al. 2014), so gambling thoughts may be held with less conviction (Toneatto et al. 2007). As noted in "Cognitive Behaviour Therapy" chapter of this book, Ladouceur (2004) found this was a difference between problem and casual gamblers.

Mindfulness may serve as a form of exposure to urges. In "urge surfing" clients are encouraged to mindfully observe the ebb and flow of urges without responding (Marlatt and Parks 1982).

Evidence that Mindfulness-Based Treatment Is Effective for Problem Gambling

Research is in early stages and includes correlational studies (de Lisle et al. 2014; Riley 2014; Reid et al. 2014; Lakey et al. 2007), case studies (Toneatto et al. 2007; De Lisle et al. 2011; Shonin et al. 2014), two pilot studies (Chen et al. 2014;

Toneatto et al. 2014), a literature review (de Lisle 2012), a review and meta-analysis (Maynard et al. 2015) and a randomised controlled trial (McIntosh et al. 2016). All these studies offer support for the use of mindfulness interventions to treat problem gamblers.

The McIntosh et al. Study: Mindfulness, Thought Suppression, Rumination and Gambling

McIntosh, Crino and O'Neill (2016) compared three treatments: (i) mindfulness intervention, (ii) manualised CBT and (iii) treatment as usual (TAU). TAU was a tailored treatment which was largely but not exclusively CBT. The design of the study – cross-lagged with repeated measures – allowed the authors to tease out the differential impact of mindfulness versus CBT on both gambling behaviour and a range of other measures, including measures of mindfulness, rumination and thought suppression, psychological distress and quality of life. Treatment-seeking problem gamblers were randomly allocated to one of three treatment sequences. After the initial three sessions –which included an assessment and brief psychoeducation about gambling – some received brief mindfulness training (four sessions) before brief CBT (four sessions), and some received brief CBT before mindfulness training. The third arm was TAU, that is, tailored treatment (eight sessions). Clients were assessed at pretreatment, crossover (or equivalent in the TAU group), posttreatment and 3 and 6 months posttreatment.

All three treatment sequences reduced problem gambling significantly and maintained these gains, although the manualised CBT group improved their gambling earlier. All three treatment sequences also reduced psychological distress. Interestingly, and perhaps inevitably, some measures of mindfulness from the Five Factors of Mindfulness Questionnaire (FFMQ) (Bohlmeijer et al. 2011) improved both with manualised CBT and mindfulness training (e.g. CBT increased the FFMQ factor "acting with awareness").

The main finding about mindfulness training was that there was a clear difference between the impact of mindfulness training compared to manualised CBT in terms of reduced rumination and thought suppression scores. Thought suppression and rumination are hypothesised to be trans-diagnostic maintaining factors in many psychological disorders (e.g. Harvey et al. 2004) including problem gambling (de Lisle et al. 2011; Riley 2014). As noted above, mindfulness training has been shown to reduce thought suppression and rumination (Creswell 2017). The results from McIntosh et al. (2016) suggest that mindfulness training may work to reduce problem gambling possibly through the mechanism of reducing rumination and thought suppression. However, even though manualised CBT did not reduce thought suppression and rumination, it did decrease problem gambling. Therefore, interventions that target thought suppression and rumination are not the only way to reduce problem gambling although such interventions may help maintain abstinence and generalise to other comorbid problems.

How Much Mindfulness Is Enough and How Much Practice Will Clients Do?

Toneatto et al. (2007) caution that not all clients are willing to make the effort to practise daily, and indeed problems with finding the time to meditate were included in the feedback in a pilot study of a mindfulness-based group for problem gamblers (Chen et al. 2014). Grow et al. (2015) found that participants in mindfulness-based relapse prevention (MBRP) treatment increased the amount of home meditation practice they did over the course duration but that their home practice declined once the course finished.

Participants may benefit despite not practising the recommended amount. De Lisle et al. (2011) describe a case study in which the client also did well (not gambling and maintaining her recovery from anxiety and depression) even though she did not continue with the prescribed 40 min of daily meditation beyond 8 weeks, preferring instead to employ the 3 min breathing space exercise. In a pilot study of mindfulness training integrated with CBT, those problem gamblers who practised at least some mindfulness practice posttreatment showed significantly better treatment outcomes than those who did not, despite not practising the full-recommended amount (Toneatto et al. 2014).

The relationship between the amount of practice and improved outcomes is not straightforward. Some authors have found, as expected, given that mindfulness is a skill, that more formal practice translates into more benefits (Carmody and Baer 2008; Crane et al. 2014; Grow et al. 2015). Others have not found this expected relationship (for a review see Vettese et al. 2009).

Furthermore, some extraordinarily brief mindfulness instructions have had an impact (admittedly in laboratory settings). Papies and her colleagues have found, for example, that even 20 min practice sessions reduced impulses to attractive food. The instructions were simply "try to imagine that thoughts are constructions of the mind which appear and disappear…try to observe thoughts as transient states of mind, try to observe reactions without suppressing them or avoiding them" (Papies et al. 2012; Papies et al. 2015). Similarly, May et al. (2015) and his colleagues have found very brief mindfulness interventions have an impact on smoking.

Thus, it is possible that mindfulness exercises in treatment sessions serve the function of behavioural experiments in those who seem to benefit without formal home practice. Another possibility is that those who improve without formal practice may have adopted a mindful way of viewing their experiences which cannot be captured by measurements of practice duration. Or, as in de Lisle's case study above, they can maintain their gains through the mindfulness-based cognitive therapy (MBCT) 3 min breathing space mindfulness exercise (Segal et al. 2002) or the SOBER mindful pause (Stop Observe Breathe Expand Respond) (Witkiewitz et al. 2005).

How much of the benefit of mindfulness is the result of practising a skill, and how much is a shift in perspective (following the experience of a mindfulness exercise in session) is unresolved. Until then, researchers should ensure that they make some attempt to assess home practice (Zgierska et al. 2009). Grow et al. (2015) suggest that booster sessions might be warranted to maintain home practice.

Mindfulness interventions require careful application. For example, caution clients against the common assumption that they should aim to empty their minds of all distractions. One pitfall to avoid is clients using mindfulness as an escape – so rather than becoming more aware, they become less aware (Roemer and Orsillo 2009). Another pitfall is unrealistic expectations, e.g. that mindfulness meditation can function as symptom relief. Sometimes mindfulness meditation involves facing difficult emotions. It may even achieve its benefits by functioning more as exposure than as relief.

Conclusion

de Lisle et al. (2012) notes that the most fundamental questions such as "what is mindfulness?" and "what are its mechanisms of action?" remain unanswered. Nonetheless, there are areas of general agreement. Although researchers have yet to agree on how mindfulness works, when it works or for whom, it is a rapidly expanding and promising area of investigation.

References

Alfonso, J. P., Caracuel, A., Delgado-Pastor, L. C., & Verdejo-Garcia, A. (2011). Combined goal management training and mindfulness meditation improve executive functions and decision-making performance in abstinent polysubstance abusers. *Drug and Alcohol Dependence, 117*, 78–81. doi:10.1016/j.drugalcdep.2010.12.05.

Andrade, J., May, J., & Kavanagh, D. (2012). Sensory imagery in craving: From cognitive psychology to new treatments for addiction. *Journal of Experimental Psychopathy, 3*(2), 127–145. doi:10.5127/jep.024611.

Bargh, J. A., & Chartrand, T. L. (1999). The unbearable automaticity of being. *American Psychologist, 54*, 452–479.

Blaszczynski, A., & Nowrer, L. (2002). A pathways model of problem and pathological gambling. *Addiction, 97*, 487–499.

Bohlmeijer, E., ten Klooster, P. M., Fledderus, M., Veehof, M., & Baer, R. (2011). Psychometric properties of the five facet mindfulness questionnaire in depressed adult and development of a short form. *Assessment, 18*(3), 308–320. doi:10.1177/1073191111408231.

Breslin, F. C., Zack, M., & McMain, S. (2002). An information-processing analysis of mindfulness: Implications for relapse prevention in the treatment of substance abuse. *Clinical Psychology: Science and Practice, 9*(3), 275–299.

Brevers, D., Cleeremans, A., Bechara, A., Greisen, M., Kornreich, C., Verbanck, P., & Noel, X. (2013). Impaired self-awareness in pathological gamblers. *Journal of Gambling Studies, 29*, 119–129. doi:10.1007/s10899-012-9292-2.

Brevers, D., Cleeremans, A., Bechara, A., Greisen, M., Kornreich, C., Verbanck, P., & Noel, X. (2014). Impaired metacognitive capacities in individuals with problem gambling. *Journal of Gambling Studies, 30*(1), 141–152. doi:10.1007/s10899-012-9348-3.

Carmody, J., & Baer, R. A. (2008). Relationships between mindfulness practice and levels of mindfulness, medical and psychological symptoms and well-being and psychological symptoms and well-being in a mindfulness-based stress reduction program. *Journal Behavioral Medicine, 31*, 23–33. doi:10.1007/s10865-007-9130-7.

Chen, P., Jindani, F., Perry, J., & Turner, N. (2014). Mindfulness and problem gambling treatment. *Asian Journal of Gambling Issues and Public Health, 4*, 2–17.

Chiesa, A., & Serretti, A. (2014). Are mindfulness-based interventions effective for substance use disorders? A systematic review of the evidence. *Substance Use and Misuse, 49*, 492–512. doi: 10.3109/10826084.2013.770027.

Crane, C., Crane, R. S., Eames, C., Fennell, M. J. V., Silverton, S., Williams, J. M. G., & Barnhofer, T. (2014). The effects of amount of home meditation practice in mindfulness based cognitive therapy on hazard to relapse to depression in the staying well after depression trial. *Behaviour Research and Therapy, 63*, 17–24. doi:10.1016/j.brat.2014.08.015.

Creswell, J. D. (2017). Mindfulness interventions. *Annual Review of Psychology, 68*, 491–516. doi:10.1146/annurev-psych-042716-051139.

Daubenmier, J., Hayden, D., Chang, V., & Epel, E. (2014). It's not what you think, it's how you relate to it: Dispositional mindfulness moderates the relationship between psychological distress and the cortisol awakening response. *Psychoneuroendocrinology, 48*, 11–18. doi:10.1016/j.psyneuen.2014.05.012.

de Lisle, S. M., Dowling, N. A., & Allen, J. S. (2011). Mindfulness-based cognitive therapy for problem gambling. *Clinical Case Studies, 10*(3), 211–228. doi:10.1177/1534650111401016.

de Lisle, S. M., Dowling, N., & Allen, J. S. (2012). Mindfulness and problem gambling: A review of the literature. *Journal of Gambling Studies, 28*, 719–739. doi:10.1007/s10899-011-9284-7.

de Lisle, S. M., Dowling, N., & Allen, J. S. (2014). Mechanisms of action in the relationship between mindfulness and problem gambling behaviour. *International Journal Mental Health and Addiction, 12*, 206–225. doi:10.1007/s11469-014-9475-4.

Dobson, K. S. (2013). The science of CBT: Toward a metacognitive model of change. *Behavior Therapy, 44*, 224–227.

Fernie, B. A., Caselli, G., Giustina, L., Donato, G., Marcotriggiani, A., & Spada, M. M. (2014). Desire thinking as a predictor of gambling. *Addictive Behaviors, 39*, 793–796. doi:10.1016/j.addbeh.2014.01.010.

Grow, J. C., Collins, S. E., Harrop, E. N., & Marlatt, G. A. (2015). Enactment of home practice following mindfulness-based relapse prevention and its association with substance-use outcomes. *Addictive Behaviors, 40*, 16–20. doi:10.1016/j.addbeh.2014.07.030.

Harvey, A. G., Watkins, E., Mansell, W., & Shafran, R. (2004). *Cognitive behavioural processes across psychological disorders: A transdiagnostic approach to research and treatment*. Oxford: Oxford University Press.

Jauregu, P., Urbiola, I., & Estevez, A. (2016). Metacognition in pathological gambling and its relationship with anxious and depressive symptomatology. *Journal Gambling Studies, 32*, 675–688. doi:10.1007/s10899-015-9552-z.

Kabat-Zinn, J. (2013). Forward. In Z. V. Segal, J. M. G. Williams, & J. D. Teasdale (Eds.), *Mindfulness-based cognitive therapy for depression*. New York: The Guilford Press.

Kavanagh, D. J., Andrade, J., & May, J. (2004). Beating the urge: Implications of research into substance-related desires. *Addictive Behaviors, 29*, 1359–1372. doi:10.1016/j.addbeh.2004.06.009.

Ladouceur, R. (2004). Perceptions among pathological and nonpathological gamblers. *Addictive Behaviors, 29*, 55–565. doi:10.1006/j.addbeh.2003.08.025.

Lakey, C. E., Campbell, W. K., Brown, K. W., & Goodie, A. S. (2007). Dispositional mindfulness as a predictor of the severity of gambling outcomes. *Personality and Individual Differences, 43*, 1698–1710. doi:10.1016/j.paid.2007.05.007.

Lindberg, A., Fernie, B. A., & Spada, M. M. (2011). Metacognitions in problem gambling. *Journal of Gambling Studies, 27*, 73–81. doi:10.1007/s10899-010-9193-1.

Mansueto, G., Pennellli, M., De Palo, V., Monacis, L., Sinatra, N., Caro, D., & M.F. (2016). The role of metacognition in pathological gambling: A mediation model. *Journal Gambling Studies, 32*, 93–106. doi:10.1007/s10899-014-9519-5.

Marlatt, G. A., & Parks, G. A. (1982). Self-management of addictive behaviors. In P. Karoly & F. H. Kanfer (Eds.), *Self-management and behaviour change*. New York: Pergamon Press.

May, J., Kavanagh, D. J., & Andrade, J. (2015). The elaborated intrusion theory of desire: A 10-year retrospective and implications for addiction treatments. *Addictive Behaviors, 44*, 29–34. doi:10.1016/j.addbeh.2014.09.016.

Maynard, B. R., Wilson, A. N., Labuzienski, E., & Whiting, S. W. (2015). Mindfulness-based approaches in the treatment of disordered gambling: A systematic review and meta-analysis. *Research on Social Work Practice, 25*, 1–15. doi:10.1177/1049731515606977.

McIntosh, C. C., Crino, R. D., & O'Neill, K. (2016). Treating problem gambling samples with cognitive behavioural therapy and mindfulness-based interventions: A clinical trial. *Journal of Gambling Studies, 32*, 1305–1325. doi:10.1007/s10899-016-9602-1.

Papies, E. K., Barsalou, L. W., & Custers, R. (2012). Mindful attention prevents mindless impulses. *Social Psychological and Personality Science, 3*(3), 291–299. doi:10.1177/1948550611419031.

Papies, E. K., Pronk, T. M., Keesman, M., & Barsalou, L. W. (2015). The benefits of simply observing: Mindful attention modulates the link between motivation and behaviour. *Journal of Personality and Social Psychology, 108*(1), 148–170. doi:10.1037/a0038032.

Raylu, N., & Oei, T. P. S. (2004). The gambling related cognitions scale (GRCS): Development, confirmatory factor validation and psychometric properties. *Addiction, 99*, 757–769. doi:10.1111/j.1360-0443.2004.00753.x.

Raylu, N., Oei, T. P. S., Loo, J. M. Y., & Tsai, J. (2016). Testing the validity of a cognitive behavioural model for gambling behaviour. *Journal Gambling Studies, 32*, 773–788. doi:10.1007/s10899-015-9567-5.

Reid, R. C., Tirro, C. D., & Fong, T. W. (2014). Mindfulness in patients with gambling disorders. *Journal of Social Work Practice in the Addictions, 14*, 327–337. doi:10.1080/1533256X.2014.958493.

Riley, B. (2014). Experiential avoidance mediates the association between thought suppression and mindfulness with problem gambling. *Journal of Gambling Studies, 30*, 163–171. doi:10.1007/s10899-012-9342-9.

Roemer, L., & Orsillo, S. M. (2009). *Mindfulness-and acceptance-based behavioural therapies in practice*. New York: The Guilford Press.

Segal, Z. V., Williams, J. M. G., & Teasdale, J. D. (2002). *Mindfulness-based cognitive therapy for depression*. New York: The Guilford Press.

Shonin, E., Van Gordon, W., & Griffiths, M. D. (2014). Cognitive behavioural therapy (CBT) and meditation awareness training (MAT) for the treatment of co-occurring schizophrenia and pathological gambling: A case study. *International Journal Mental Health and Addiciton, 12*, 181–196. doi:10.1007/s11469-013-9460-3.

Spada, M. M., Caselli, G., & Wells, A. (2012). The metacognitive therapy approach to problem drinking. In S. C. Hayes & M. E. Levin (Eds.), *Mindfulness and acceptance for addictive behaviors*. Oakland CA: New Harbinger Publications.

Spada, M. M., Caselli, G., Nikcevic, A. V., & Wells, A. (2015). Metacognition in addictive behaviors. *Addictive Behaviors, 44*, 9–15. doi:10.1016/j.addbeh.2014.08.002.

Spada, M. M., Guistina, L., Rolandi, S., Fernie, B. A., & Caselli, G. (2014). Profiling metacognition in gambling disorder. *Behavioural and Cognitive Psychotherapy, 43*, 614–622. doi:10.1017/S1352465814000101.

Stott, R., Mansell, W., Salkovskis, P., Lavender, A., & Cartwright-Hatton, S. (2010). *Oxford guide to metaphors in CBT*. Oxford: Oxford University Press.

Toneatto, T. (1995). The regulation of cognitive states: A cognitive model of psychoactive substance abuse. *Journal of Cognitive Psychotherapy: An International Quarterly, 9*(2), 93–104.

Toneatto, T. (1999a). A metacognitive analysis of craving: Implications for treatment. *Journal of Clinical Psychology, 55*(5), 527–537.

Toneatto, T. (1999b). Metacognition and substance use. *Addictive Behaviors, 24*(2), 167–174.

Toneatto, T., Pillai, S., & Courtice, E. L. (2014). Mindfulness-enhanced cognitive behaviour therapy for problem gamblers: A controlled pilot study. *International Journal Mental Health and Addiction, 12*, 197–205. doi:10.1007/s11469-014-9481-6.

Toneatto, T., Vettese, L., & Nguyen, L. (2007). The role of mindfulness in the cognitive-behavioural treatment of problem gambling. *Journal of Gambling Issues, 19*, 91–100.

Vettese, L. C., Toneatto, T., Stea, J. N., Nguyen, L., & Wang, J. J. (2009). Do mindfulness meditation participants do their homework? And does it make a difference? A review of the empirical evidence. *Journal of Cognitive Psychotherapy: An International Quarterly, 23*(3), 198–225. doi:10.1891/0889-8391.23.3.198.

Wells, A. (2000). *Cognitive therapy of anxiety disorders: A practice manual and conceptual guide*. Chichester: Wiley.

Wells, A., & Cartwright-Hatton, S. (2004). A short form of the metacognitions questionnaire: Properties of the MCQ-30. *Behaviour Research and Therapy, 42*(4), 385–396. doi:10.1016/S0005-7967(03)00147-5.

Williams, J. M. G. (2010). Mindfulness and psychological process. *Emotion, 10*(1), 1–7. doi:10.1037/a0018360.

Witkiewitz, K., Marlatt, G. A., & Walker, D. (2005). Mindfulness-based relapse prevention for alcohol and substance use disorders. *Journal of Cognitive Psychotherapy: An international quarterly, 19*(3), 211–228.

Zgierska, A., Rabago, D., Chawla, N., Kushner, K., Koehler, R., & Marlatt, A. (2009). Mindfulness meditation for substance use disorders: A systematic review. *Substance Abuse, 30*, 266–294. doi:10.1080/08897070903250019.

Chapter 6
Schema Therapy for Problem Gamblers

Cameron McIntosh

CBT remains the most effective treatment for PG (PGRTC 2011). Yet, scope remains for improvements to both the short- and long-term effectiveness for treatment-seeking PGs (Rickwood et al. 2010). Alternative or adjunctive treatments to CBT should be considered to address the above treatment effectiveness gaps. This chapter explores schema therapy as an adjunct to CBT for PG.

What Is Schema Therapy and Why Might It Be Helpful for PGs?

Schema therapy was originally developed by Jeffrey Young (1990, 1999) to treat patients with characterological problems that manifested in entrenched, chronic psychological disorders that did not respond to traditional CBT. Blaszczynski and Nower's (2002) Pathways Model identified anti-social personality traits as forming one of the three routes into PG, suggesting a role for schema therapy for those members of the PG population whose anti-social personality characteristics led to and maintain their PG.

Recently, the schema mode approach (SMA) has expanded traditional schema therapy. Young defined early maladaptive schemas (EMSs) as self-defeating cognitive and emotional patterns that begin early in development and repeat throughout life (Young 1990, 1999). He defined schema modes as a set of currently active schemas or schema operations that can be adaptive or maladaptive (Young et al. 2003). These modes can be persistent or shift frequently, are divided into mostly

C. McIntosh (✉)
St Vincent's Hospital Gambling Treatment Program, St Vincent's Hospital, 390 Victoria St, Darlinghurst, Sydney, NSW 2010, Australia
e-mail: cameron@uniqueminds.com.au

C. McIntosh, K. O'Neill, *Evidence-Based Treatments for Problem Gambling*, SpringerBriefs in Psychology, DOI 10.1007/978-3-319-62485-3_6

negative emotions, and other modes may be developed and used to cope with the negative emotions. SMA asserts that these modes may be more effectively identified and changed than the underlying schemas (Arntz and Jacob. 2013).

SMA provides an appealing heuristic for explaining the maintenance of PG behaviour, particularly for patients whose symptoms persist despite actively completing CBT for PG programmes. We believe that SMA may also be appropriate for patients presenting via the emotionally vulnerable as well as via the anti-social personality disordered pathway (Blaszczynski and Nower 2002). Our anecdotal experience suggests that the SMA heuristic is well accepted by PGs and the ensuing treatment has been effectively deployed to a small number of PGs in our clinic. Robust research on SMA approach for PG is the next step.

What Is Schema Therapy?

CBT was described by Young et al. (2003) as being based on the following assumptions that limited its usefulness for entrenched, chronic psychological disorders: patients are motivated to build skills, complete homework and solve problems and are capable of change with prodding and positive reinforcement, and they will comply with treatment protocols; patients can access cognitions and emotions and report them easily to the therapist; cognitions and behaviours will change via empirical analysis, experimentation, logical discourse and repetition; patients have a degree of psychological flexibility that allows them to respond to treatment in a relative short period of time; the therapeutic relationship is established early and easily and is not a focal ingredient of treatment.

As clinicians treating PG know, treatment-seeking PGs do not always act in a way that is consistent with the above descriptions. PG can present as entrenched, resistant over longer periods to CBT treatment, and is sometimes formulated to be a response to intense emotional distress that has origins earlier in patient's lives than when they present for treatment. Schema therapy has obvious appeal for treating such PGs given its focus on reducing the impact of childhood and adolescent origins of psychological problems and that it is now seen as flexible to patient needs in terms of the length of time in treatment (Young et al. 2003).

Early Maladaptive Schemas

Young (1990) proposed a classification system of common schemas that underlie individual psychopathology. To this end, he developed the Young Schema Questionnaire (YSQ; Young 1990; Young and Brown 2001) consisting of 205 items that attempted to assess 16 core themes thought to be common to psychopathology. Subsequent research has resulted in a further two schemas being identified and a

Table 6.1 Early maladaptive schema domains and early maladaptive schemas

EMS domain	EMS
Disconnection and rejection	Abandonment/instability; mistrust/abuse; emotional deprivation; defectiveness/shame; social isolation/alienation
Impaired autonomy and achievement	Dependency/incompetency; vulnerability to harm and illness; enmeshment/undeveloped self; failure
Impaired limits	Entitlement/grandiosity; lack of self-control/self-discipline
Other-directedness	Subjugation; self-sacrifice; approval seeking
Hypervigilance and inhibition	Negativity/pessimism; emotional inhibition; unrelenting standards; punitiveness

Table 6.2 Early maladaptive schemas (Arntz and Jacob. 2013)

EMS domain	Basic need
Disconnection and rejection	Safe attachment, acceptance, care
Impaired autonomy and achievement	Autonomy, competence, sense of identity
Impaired limits	Realistic limits, self-control
Other-directedness	Free expression of needs and emotions
Hypervigilance and inhibition	Spontaneity, playfulness

shortened 90-item version (YSQ-SF; Young 2005) that has returned respectable validity (Scott and Crino 2014). The 18 EMS currently identified are listed in Table 6.1 (from Arntz and Jacob 2013).

Early maladaptive schemas (EMSs) are believed to develop when basic childhood needs are not adequately met. The resulting dysfunction takes the form of restrictions on recognising, fulfilling and experiencing needs in later life. Both the EMSs themselves and the processes that have formed in childhood to adapt to the absence of the needs being met are thought to contribute to dysfunction. For example, a child whose parents separate in acrimonious circumstances may fail to have their attachment, security and safety needs met. Later in life, difficulties with stable relationship forming and coping strategies including prematurely ending relationships due to perceptions of mistrust may occur.

The basic human needs as defined by Young et al. (2003) fall into five groups, each mapping to an EMS domain. Both the EMS domains and the basic needs were developed from clinical observation rather than strict experimental designs, explaining why new EMSs have been identified and added to the schema therapy model over time. Current EMS domains and the corresponding unmet human needs are set out in Table 6.2.

Although the identification of an individual's EMS is best obtained by clinical observation/judgement, there are a number of instruments with reasonable psychometric properties that can be used to supplement that process. The YSQ-SF (Young 2005) and Schema Modes Inventory (Lobbestael et al. 2010) are our preferred 'user friendly' instruments given their validity and lower patient burden than the original YSQ.

What Is the Schema Mode Approach?

Many PGs report that they are unable to explain 'what comes over them' in the period before and during their disordered gambling. For example, patients have reported to us that they 'lose their mind' and that they engage in gambling even though they understand the odds of them winning are very low. They also report recognising that the damage they are exposing themselves to in terms of interpersonal conflict, financial distress and unhealthy behaviour likely has long-term consequences. The 'felt' or emotional experience that accompanies the period prior to and during gambling activities can be under-explored in CBT, when conceptualising that process as automatic or if focused on primarily cognitive functions. These experiences may better be conceptualised for some PGs as reflecting the operation of schema modes.

Originally developed by Young et al. (2003) and developed further by Lobbestael et al. (2009), the schema mode approach seeks to explain the psychological distress arising from the conflict between different 'parts/sides' of an individual. SMA sees current triggering situations as activating a very specific memory or memories associated with an intensely distressing emotional experience, from a key developmental period, similar to the maintenance of a trauma memory network (Foa et al. 1989; Brockman and Calvert 2016). Contemporary attempts to respond to the psychological distress created by the triggering situation are sought from representations of key developmental figures that were present earlier in life (parent modes) or via the cognitive processes available to the patient at the younger age (child modes).

In addition to the development of the parent and child modes, an individual may activate schema coping modes to provide the best working solution to the distress they are experiencing. Reinforcement, for example in the form of reduced distress, may serve to further embed the validity of the mode(s). The operation of the mode pattern is a poorer substitute for one or more of the childhood needs not having been met. The schema coping modes may be accompanied by lower levels of emotional intensity than the other modes. Unlike the other modes, the reported 'felt' age of the individual when they are experiencing the coping mode tends to be aligned with their actual age rather than the age at which the unmet need presented as initially being problematic (Arntz and Jacob 2013).

The schema coping modes are believed to fall into three distinct categories. Individuals may have preferred or persistent coping styles, or the behavioural and experiential patterns may move, between the coping styles. The three categories of the schema coping modes are:

- Surrender – the schema is taken as accurate and the patient gives in to the maladaptive parts of the schema.
- Avoidance – the situation(s) triggering the schema is avoided to circumvent the intense emotions associated when triggered.
- Overcompensation – acting in a dominant way opposite to the maladaptive parts of the schema.

Table 6.3 Expanded schema modes (Arntz and Jacob. 2013)

Dysfunctional child modes – lonely, angry, abandoned/abused, dependent, enraged, obstinate, impulsive, undisciplined		
Dysfunctional parent modes – punitive and demanding		
Coping modes	Surrender	Compliant surrenderer
	Avoidance	Detached protector; avoidant protector; angry protector; detached self-soother
	Overcompensation	Self-aggrandiser; attention-seeking mode; perfectionistic/overcontroller; paranoid overcontroller; bully and attack; conning and manipulative; predator
	Functional or healthy modes	Happy child; healthy adult

The schema modes have been expanded recently as described below (Table 6.3).

It is very helpful to firstly identify which of the three broad modes is operating within the formulation. Child modes relate to feelings consistent with a much younger age than the patient actually is, such as being overwhelmed, highly stressed or abandoned or experiencing a deep sense of threat. Enraged and impulsive feelings are also possible in the child modes. In gambling patients, a sense of lacking discipline, poor limit setting skills and the absence of an appropriate role model who can process difficult emotional states is common. We have seen both the vulnerable and the angry child modes in our clinic, the latter being associated with 'tantrum'-like behaviour when no other strategy reduces the distressing feelings. Gambling excessively/inappropriately is then used as a fraught way of working around the unmet needs.

The dysfunctional parent modes are characterised by self-hate, high pressure and overbearingness (Johnson et al. 2006). They are distinct from the child modes in that they are secondary and are believed to represent constructions within the patient of their caregiver's morality and behaviour. Punitive parent mode is the common expression of high moral values. The demanding parent reflects high pressure and maintenance of standards to achieve perfection and to do better than others (Arntz and Jacob. 2013). This mode presents commonly in our clinic alongside generalised anxiety disorder.

The schema mode approach allows the therapist to work with the patient to map out the maladaptive process that follows once an EMS has been triggered and to identify adaptive ways in which to get the patient's needs met. SMA involves working in the present, as well as appreciating the times at which the EMS was formed or reinforced. It involves designing effective ways for operating in the future. It is familiar in many ways to CBT treatment and therefore it aligns well as an adjunct to CBT.

What Is the Broader Evidence for the Schema Mode Approach?

SMA has also been reported to reduce symptoms in non-personality disordered populations for psychopathology such as depression (Renner et al. 2016). Depression appears commonly co-morbid with PG (Petry 2005). Whilst no specific research has yet examined the use of SMA for treating PG, support for SMA treatments in broader personality disordered individuals suffering from PG and PGs with mood disorders could be a good initial subset to target. This may be particularly relevant for those patients in the above subset whose recovery is resistant to CBT or for whom CBT does not provide a longer-term positive treatment outcome.

Cognitive and Behavioural Interventions in SMA

Cognitive interventions in PG treatment are typically used to strengthen an individual's understanding of the risk that gambling presents for them, to raise awareness of thinking patterns that are maladaptive and to learn to challenge or accept potentially damaging cycles of thinking that can lead to acting in maladaptive ways. Likewise, behavioural interventions can be very helpful in limiting exposure to high-risk situations and in building constructive patterns for greater wellbeing away from the damaging behaviour. When CBT is delivered in its most narrow form, there is potential for the emotional experience to be examined in a cognitive and logical fashion. The emotional focus of schema therapy is more explicit about emotions, and techniques such as 'affect bridges' and 'limited reparenting' (see below) are used.

Schema Mode Interventions

A number of schema mode interventions that we have used in the treatment of PGs are discussed below using the case study of a patient called Audrey.

Case Study

Audrey was a medical professional who reported gambling extensively for 10 years using online poker machines, often losing her entire fortnightly salary. She reported a number of longstanding interpersonal conflicts with key colleagues at work, and the major gambling events would occur after distressing interactions with these colleagues. She had few social contacts outside of her work, and her marriage had deteriorated to the point of a divorce 3 years prior to assessment. She presented as highly organised, and she attended with a range of articles she had sourced on PG treatment. She described many examples in which colleagues had breached company conventions and became defensive when her interpretation of events was explored and challenged. Audrey stated that during her teenage years she would focus intently on her studies and would restrict her eating when her standards were not met by herself or others.

Assessment Audrey's YSQ-SF revealed scores of 5+ for items related to unrelenting standards, emotional inhibition (both hypervigilance and inhibition schema domains) and mistrust abuse (disconnection and rejection). These findings were consistent with the clinical evaluation. The assessment revealed Audrey's father left the family when she was 10 years old and moved to another state with a new partner, severing contact for 5 years. Audrey stated that her mother insisted that she always be well groomed when leaving the house and stressed the importance of having a stable career so as to achieve independence. Audrey also reported that she felt most satisfied in life when she worked in research assistant roles where protocols were used for clinical trials. Since the rising to the team leader role 10 years earlier, she had experienced greater conflict and had increased her use of online poker machines which she accessed via her desktop computer at home. We also assessed her childhood unmet needs, EMSs and modes using an 'affect bridge' (see below).

The assessment was completed using clinical interviews over three sessions, and the clinical findings were validated using the following instruments: Young Schema Questionnaire Short Form (Young 2005), Schema Modes Inventory (Lobbestael et al. 2010), Depression Anxiety and Stress Scale-21 item (Lovibond and Lovibond 1995) and the Problem Gambling Severity Index (PGSI; Ferris and Wynne 2001). Homework during the assessment phase consisted of implementing stimulus control measures to restrict access to money and her computer at home, monitoring of urges, behavioural activation and scheduling adaptive behaviours.

Case conceptualisation The case conceptualisation process was iterative over two sessions. The therapist focused on presenting the draft to her after the assessment and validity testing to achieve agreement, consistent with CBT. Psychoeducation about each of the modes, learning theory relevant to PG and CBT-based practices such as accurate information on the chances of winning and benefits of stimulus control were also weaved into the sessions at this time.

In the next phase of treatment, we explained the basic childhood needs (Table 6.2 above) and discussed examples of the dysfunction in the hypervigilance/inhibition and disconnection/rejections schema domains. A further level of detail was then provided in terms of the specific EMSs identified in the assessment. Amendments were made throughout to the case conceptualisation to keep it current and meaningful. Homework activities were set from Young and Klosko (1994) (Fig. 6.1).

SMA psychoeducation The next stage involved a deeper exploration of the formation of the EMSs. 'Affect bridges' were used to make the learnings experiential. The parent and child modes were introduced, as was the distress that she felt when they

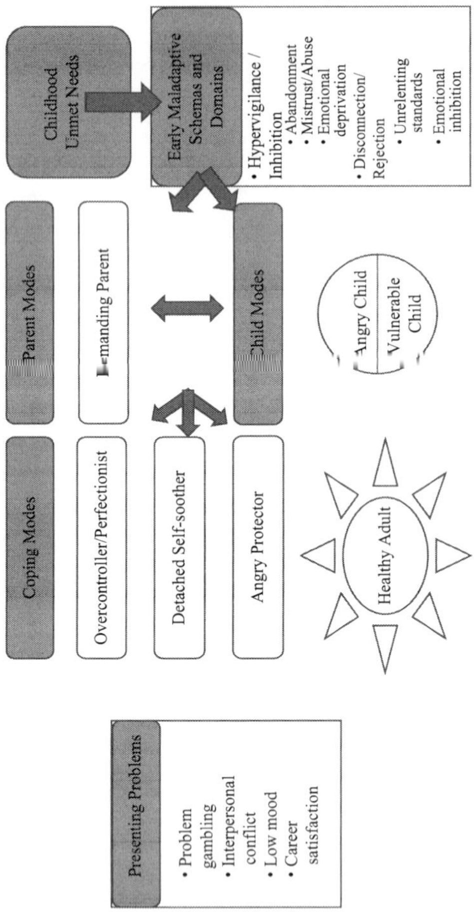

Fig. 6.1 Case conceptualisation for Audrey

were activated by a situation in the present. We found it relevant here to tie the 'voices' or instructions these modes delivered to her in distressing times to the relevant mode. For Audrey, the demanding parent voice was easily assignable to her mother and the vulnerable child voice was herself around 13 years of age.

Audrey found the description of the modes more 'palatable' when we referred to them as 'sides' of herself that were in control at different times. Of particular note in Audrey's conceptualisation was the distress she experienced from the interaction of the parent and child modes once the EMSs were activated. We agreed that the tension between those modes was often unresolved and lead to the use of coping modes to relieve the distress.

After two sessions on the parent and child modes, the relevant coping modes were introduced under the broad categories of surrender, overcompensation and avoidance. 'Affect bridges' were used again over a number of sessions so that Audrey developed a cognitive and emotional understanding of the differences between the modes. Healthy adult mode was introduced early in the treatment phase as an effective way of getting needs met. Homework was given throughout to monitor the hardest and best parts of each day, and then for the above conceptualisation to be used to identify which modes were operating at those times.

Audrey was also asked to note more details about the modes as they occurred in her day to day life for homework We were particularly keen for her to focus on the 'felt' aspects, so she developed greater skills recognising the differences between the modes, again in both a cognitive and emotional way. One goal was for her to see the modes as independent 'sides' of herself that could be isolated, identified and explained as states rather than traits.

After Audrey had developed a good working understanding of all of the different modes, further psychoeducation about the limbic system with visual aids was provided. Here we explained the activation of this system as being triggered when contemporary situations aroused distressing memories stored in the hippocampus. Pros and cons of the various modes were worked through to demonstrate that there were positive aspects to each of them, where the limitations existed and what costs were involved in allowing the modes to operate unchallenged. The healthy adult mode was highlighted as incorporating many of the positive aspects of the maladaptive schemas, so change was both desirable and achievable.

Chair work and imagery rescripting After ten sessions, treatment then moved on to using 'chair work' and 'imagery rescripting'. Chair work operates in both the cognitive and emotional-focused treatment domains. This process involved separating Audrey's modes, and over various sessions allocating individual chairs for each mode. In the earlier sessions, only the modes that were being worked upon in that session were allocated chairs, for example, the parent and child modes were isolated to establish the nature of the conflict between those modes, before exploring the coping modes.

The therapist and Audrey took turns either playing the individual modes or interacting with them from another modes' perspective. When 'playing' a mode the relevant person would sit in the chair designated for that mode, and when shifting to another mode physical movement to the other relevant chair was required. Awareness, acceptance and challenge of the modes were key in chair work, so that Audrey could develop skills in properly identifying and meeting the needs of each mode rather than operating in the dysfunctional automatic way that had caused problems in the past. For example, when the demanding parent mode placed more pressure on the vulnerable child to do better as a means of resolving distress, the needs of the vulnerable child were elicited and advice from the healthy adult mode was sought.

Imagery rescripting (Arntz et al. 2007) was introduced in later sessions to help Audrey address schema-related problems. The use of imagery in CBT is well established (Hackman et al. 2011; Holmes and Mathews 2005; Hunt and Fenton 2007). Audrey was asked to recount a recent distressing situation she had encountered at work. After a brief summary, we asked Audrey to close her eyes, relax her body and try to access the memory of the distressing situation as if she was re-experiencing it. She was directed to put her attention a few moments in time prior to the peak of distress in the imagined scenario. Audrey was asked to explain details of the environment in the first person, and as the detail built, she was asked to explain how she felt. Audrey described her feelings from a factual rather than 'felt' perspective initially, so we slowed down her account and focused on getting more emotional and physical sensations detail about her experience in the scenario. Audrey found it helpful to use metaphors to describe her feelings, for example 'I feel like I'm a trapped and injured animal and the only way for me to deal with this situation is to come out fighting'. Once the emotions and sensations were described in more detail, we helped Audrey move forward in her account and asked her to maintain focus on her 'felt' experience as she progressed to the key point of distress. We also asked her to note any changes she noticed in her emotional experience as she progressed through her account of the past distressing experience. Unlike an exposure and response prevention protocol, we were not trying to elevate Audrey's distress and then to allow habituation, rather we wanted her to activate the schema modes to a level she could recognise their character in a more detailed way.

Once the above was achieved, we asked Audrey to reflect on a childhood memory where she had felt a similar cluster of emotions. The above process is called an 'affect bridge', which helps link the 'felt' contemporary distressing experience to a period earlier in life when the EMS may have been formed. Audrey stated that a memory of her at age 13 presented itself, in which she was frightened because she was not picked up from a hockey training session by her mother after dark. When her mother finally did turn up, she berated Audrey for standing in the wrong spot, breaching a rule about never being alone after dark and that she had put herself at great risk of physical harm and her mother all out of schedule with her own commitments. In the memory, Audrey's mother did not acknowledge her fear and made no attempt to comfort her, rather she increased her distress by blaming her for the situation.

We elicited Audrey's feelings in detail and then asked her to visualise the therapist in the imagined scenario at her house after being driven home by her mother. The therapist then 'rescripted' the memory to facilitate the creation of new and more functional memories. In the new script, the therapist comforted Audrey, and sought to resolve the conflict Audrey felt about not being able to act in a way that would have met her mother's standards. One goal was to help Audrey feel safe, and to open Audrey's interpretation to the idea that sometimes mistakes occur and searching for the person to blame is often not going to meet anybody's needs. In the image we also spoke to Audrey's mother to try and facilitate learning for her, and the negative consequences that can occur when Audrey's mother's anxiety leads to berating Audrey, rather than teaching her how to stay safe when things go wrong. The focus was on empathetically challenging Audrey's mother about her behaviour so that Audrey's needs of attachment, safety, care and spontaneity and play were met. This process was repeated for a number of distressing memories in which Audrey's needs were not met. Such a process is known as 'limited reparenting'.

Final Comments on Treatment

Throughout treatment, learning to spend more time in the healthy adult mode when triggering situations occurred was a broad goal. The individualised case conceptualisation included the treatment goals: abstaining from gambling, increasing appropriate socialising in healthy environments, completing a physical accomplishment, building relationships with specific family members and pursuing a career objective. These goals helped tie the conceptualisation to the presenting problem. Within the conceptualisation, it was important to set out linkages between the unmet needs, EMSs and the parent/child/coping modes. A balance between working to directly address issues in the conceptualisation and more immediate or day-to-day concerns was managed, consistent with CBT.

A strong and productive therapeutic relationship is required in schema therapy and SMA given the need to re-parent the unmet needs not only outside the sessions but also at the times they occur in sessions. Opportunities to model effective interactions should be taken by the therapist as they arise. For example, it was helpful to explain to Audrey the impact of her behaviours on the therapist in an appropriate empathic way that showed genuine care and flexibility and to set clear, effective working boundaries with her. The therapist also needed to validate and care for her needs as they moved between the different modes, from providing safety and support for the vulnerable child to empathetic confrontation when in some of the coping modes (Arntz and Jacob. 2013).

References

Arntz, A., & Jacob., G. (2013). *Schema therapy in practice: An introductory guide to the schema mode approach*. Wiley-Blackwell: Chichester, West Sussex.

Arntz, A., Tiesema, M., & Kindt, M. (2007). Treatment of PTSD: A comparison of imaginal exposure with and without imagery rescripting. *Journal of Behaviour Therapy and Experimental Psychiatry, 38*, 345–370.

Blaszczynski, A., & Nower, L. (2002). A pathways model for problem and pathological gambling. *Addiction, 97*(5), 487–499.

Brockman, R. N., & Calvert, F. L. (2016). Imagery rescripting for PTSD and personality disorders: Theory and application. *Journal of Contemporary Psychotherapy, 47*(1), 23–30. doi:10.1007/s10879-016-9329-4.

Ferris, J., & Wynne, H. (2001). *The Canadian problem gambling index*. Ottawa: Canadian Centre on Substance Abuse.

Foa, E. B., Steketee, G., & Rothbaum, B. O. (1989). Behavioral/cognitive conceptualizations of post-traumatic stress disorder. *Behavior Therapy, 20*, 155–176.

Hackman, A., Bennett-Levy, J., & Holmes, E. A. (2011). *The oxford guide to imagery in cognitive therapy*. Oxford: Oxford University Press.

Holmes, E. A., & Mathews, A. (2005). Mental imagery and emotion: A special relationship? *Emotion, 5*, 489–497.

Holmes, E. A., Arntz, A., & Smucker, M. R. (2007). Imagery rescripting in cognitive behaviour therapy: Images, treatment techniques and outcomes. *Journal of Behavior Therapy and Experimental Psychiatry, 38*, 297–305.

Hunt, M., & Fenton, M. (2007). Imagery rescripting versus in vivo exposure in the treatment of snake fear. *Journal of Behavior Therapy and Experimental Psychiatry, 38*, 329–344.

Johnson, J. G., Cohen, P., Chen, H., Kasen, S., & Brooks, J. S. (2006). Parenting behaviors associated with the risk for offspring personality disorder during adulthood. *Archives of General Psychiatry, 63*, 579–587.

Lobbestael, J., Arntz, A., & Bernstein, D. P. (2009). Disentangling the relationship between different types of childhood maltreatment and personality disorders. *Journal of Personality Disorders, 2*[illegible](3), 28[illegible]–[illegible].

Lobbestael, J., van Vreeswijk, M., Spinhoven, P., Schouten, E., & Arntz, A. (2010). Reliability and validity of the short schema mode Inventory (SMI). *Behavioural and Cognitive Psychotherapy, 38*, 437–458.

Lovibond, S. H., & Lovibond, P. F. (1995). *Manual for the depression anxiety stress scales*. Sydney: Psychology Foundation.

Petry. (2005). *Pathological gambling: Etiology, comorbidity, and treatment*. USA: American Psychological Association.

Problem Gambling Reseach & Treatment Centre. (2011). Guideline for Screening, Assessment and Treatment of Problem Gambling. Clayton: Monash University. Productivity Commission (2010). Gambling. Productivity Commission Inquiry Report. Volume 1. Report no. 50. Canberra: Productivity Commission.

Rickwood, D., Blaszczynski, A. Delfabbro, P., Dowling, N., Heading, K. (2010). The Psychology of Gambling APS Review Paper: Australian Psychological Society.

Renner, F., Arntz, A., Peeters, F. P. M. L., Lobbestael, J., & Huibers, M. J. H. (2016). Schema therapy for chronic depression: Results of a multiple single case series. *Journal of Behavior Therapy and Experimental Psychiatry, 51*, 66–73. doi:10.1016/j.jbtep.2015.12.001.

Scott, S., & Crino, R. D. (2014). Early maladaptive schema and social and occupational functioning: The mediating role of psychiatric symptomatology. *Australian Journal of Psychology, 66*(4), 224–232. doi:10.1111/ajpy.12061.

Young, J. E. (1990). *Cognitive therapy for personality disorders: A schema-focused approach*. Sarasota, Fl: Professional Resource Press.

Young, J. E. (1999). *Cognitive therapy for personality disorders: A schema-focused approach (revised edition)*. Sarasota, Fl: Professional Resource Press.

Young, J. E. (2005). .The young schema questionnaire: Short form. Available in electronic form at http://home.sprynet.com/sprynet/schema/ysqs1.htm.

Young, J. E., & Brown, G. (1990). *Young schema questionnaire*. New York: Cognitive Therapy Centre of New York.

Young, J. E., & Brown, G. (2001). *Young schema questionnaire* (Special ed.). New York: Schema Therapy Institute.

Young, J. E., & Klosko, J. S. (1994). *Reinventing your life*. New York: Plume Books.

Young, J. E., Klosko, J. S., & Weishaar, M. E. (2003). *Schema therapy: A Practitioner's guide*. New York: Guilford.

Chapter 7
Acceptance and Commitment Therapy ("ACT") for Problem Gambling

Cameron McIntosh

Acceptance and commitment therapy (ACT; Hayes et al. 1999; Hayes and Strosahl 2005) is a behavioural treatment that was developed by Steven Hayes and is classified as one of the earlier 'third wave' psychological therapies. Third wave therapies are characterised by the inclusion of mindfulness interventions that can be used with the behavioural and cognitive treatments from the earlier two behavioural and cognitive waves. The treatment effectiveness of ACT for psychopathology that is commonly comorbid with PG, such as mood, substance misuse, and anxiety disorders has been documented (Ruiz 2012; Harris 2006). Some preliminary studies exploring ACT as a treatment for PG have also been reported (Dixon et al. 2016). This chapter provides the background to ACT, reports its current use for PG, and explores possible future uses for the PG population as demonstrated using a treatment case study undertaken at our clinic.

ACT theorists see the suffering we experience from painful events, such as loss, unexpected upset, and physically painfully experiences, as being amplified because of the way we interpret those events, rather than due solely to the events themselves. Inherent in the way that we interpret these events are our verbal abilities. Relational frame theory (RFT; Hayes et al. 2001) seeks to explain the importance of our verbal abilities in the above process and underpins ACT. RFT asserts that the relationships we interpret as existing between events are mostly formed as children and/or are built on social convention, rather than simply being based upon the physical properties of the events in front of us at any given time.

RFT states that the relationships between events develop as we age, creating a larger relational network of socially or culturally derived modes of living. Such a network is hypothesised to operate automatically in the background, structuring our world.

C. McIntosh (✉)
St Vincent's Hospital Gambling Treatment Program, St Vincent's Hospital,
390 Victoria St, Darlinghurst, Sydney, NSW 2010, Australia
e-mail: cameron@uniqueminds.com.au

C. McIntosh, K. O'Neill, *Evidence-Based Treatments for Problem Gambling*,
SpringerBriefs in Psychology, DOI 10.1007/978-3-319-62485-3_7

Fig. 7.1 ACT hexaflex containing the six core processes

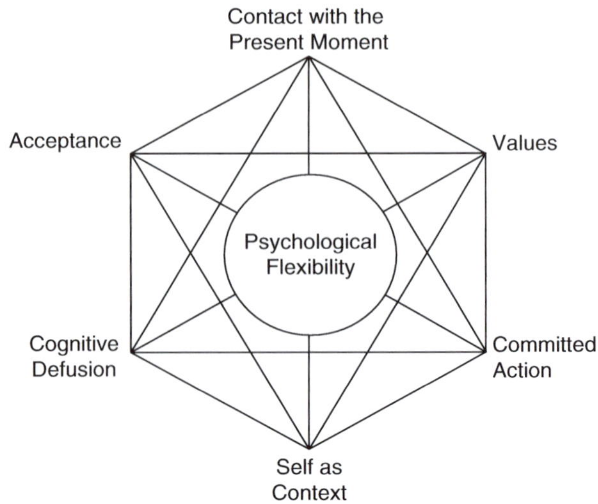

Such a process can be maladaptive to a particular situation when the interpretation is automatic and not nuanced to the current situation can lead our interpretations to be maladaptive.

ACT is the therapeutic application of RFT that is designed to help patients develop greater levels of psychological flexibility (Louma et al. 2007). Increased flexibility in psychological processing may counteract the negative impacts arising from the automatic operation of the relational network described above. The processes in ACT that promote psychological flexibility are discussed below.

The overarching goal in ACT is to help patients be open to and willing to have their inner experiences whilst focusing attention on living a meaningful or value-consistent life, not on trying to escape or avoid pain. We have observed many cases where PGs have become overwhelmed with efforts to enable their gambling and maintain a perception of normality in other aspects of their life, and in the process they have sacrificed the pursuit of their values. Some examples include PGs who have stolen from their employers to fund their PG and set up elaborate over-confident behaviours that mislead their employer and their relatives, whilst gambling, and missing key family events. In these examples, the effort required to maintain the above deceit and the time spent gambling resulted in major diversions from their value-based living, which included connection with others, wisdom, and loyalty.

Core Therapeutic Processes

The six core therapeutic processes in ACT are designed to assist patients achieve greater levels of psychological flexibility. The core processes are outlined on the ACT hexaflex, which is contained in Fig. 7.1.

The six core processes are summarised briefly below (Hayes et al. 2005):

Acceptance Acceptance is positioned as a preferred alternative to experiential avoidance. For example, many of our PG patients become distressed when they experience urges to gamble. They report that the presence of the urge in their thoughts carries with it a requirement to act on the urge, as that action will make the distress reduce in the short term. Acceptance in this context involves assisting the patient to increase their active awareness and tolerance of the experience of having gambling urges, without seeking to change their form or frequency. For example, some PGs are able to 'let go' of the drive to reduce their distress by negative actions when they are taught to take a position of observation and noting of the component parts of their distressing experience. Such a process then reduces the 'battle' between their long-standing historical agenda of trying to control or rid themselves of the unwanted urge and associated shameful feelings attached to the negative actions.

Cognitive Defusion Cognitive Defusion relies on the principle from RFT that the efforts to rid ourselves of unwanted private experiences increase distress within the relational network. The distress created then serves to make the 'event' (often in the form of a feeling or emotion) more important. Such a process is believed to narrow the behavioural repertoire, because the events are often connected to a rich historical network that is automatically activated, and reliance on this process is attached to a well-established reinforced pattern. The therapists in our clinic assist patients to see that alternatives to the automatic processes are available when they openly and willingly experience the urges. This approach provides a platform for new learning and ultimately involves less psychological distress than trying to avoid experiencing the gambling urge at all. Education is provided about learning theory to explain that urges may be triggered by an association with a mood state, time of day, or location, nothing more. That is, even though the experience is distressing the importance of the content in the message may be nothing more than an artefact, so current relevant information to the situation may deserve more weighting in the interpretation.

Defusion involves the process of understanding thoughts from a more useful perspective than the literal meaning of the words used to describe them. Defusion is concerned with reducing the largely automatic, unintended, and historical process of relating one event to another so that values can be introduced as an alternative more conscious approach of directing behaviour (Louma et al. 2007). Such a process facilitates the interpretation of the words in the form relevant to the current situation, not as what they mean more broadly in society or have meant to an individual in the past. For PGs, practicing defusion is promoted to create a looser relationship with the urge to gamble experience and to encourage greater flexibility of behaviour, that is, to make more adaptive and situationally relevant choices.

Self as Context Self as Context is largely concerned with raising awareness of the interpretations that we have developed about ourselves and built as we have grown up. Societal beliefs and experiences over our life create a sense of who each of us are in our own understanding. For example, 'I am smart', 'I am dumb,' or 'I am an impulsive person who has poor discipline and difficulty acting like a supportive parent/partner'. There are often images, thoughts, and behaviours that support the conceptualisation of our identity. The same processes that build identity can trap our PG patients into destructive behaviours so that problematic patterns of living are maintained. ACT can help to decrease attachment to the maladaptive parts of the patient's conceptualised self, create a safe platform from which defusion and acceptance work can be deployed, and promote greater flexibility in the patient's interpretation of themselves (Louma et al. 2007).

Contact with the present moment Present moment awareness places attention on the learning opportunities afforded in the current situation. Such awareness can lead to enhanced flexibility, responsiveness, and access to the greatest number of learning opportunities. The alternative to present moment focus is attention resting in the past or future. Attention outside the present moment facilitates activation of the logical/rational drive of language and the relational framework that is in place. The activation leads to a greater vulnerability that maladaptive behaviours may re-emerge, via fusion or experiential avoidance. The theory establishing contact with the present moment as a useful ACT process does not deny the importance of reflection on past situations and planning for future events is a valuable part of life. Rather it states that individuals with problematic behaviours, such as PG, will have more choice and better outcomes if they have contact with the present moment at the times they experience an urge, and will be more productive and suffer less if they direct the planning or reflection process, rather than be held prisoner to the whims of their unconscious attention as it decides where to focus. A present moment focus is encouraged when urges appear, as well as at other times wellbeing is at risk, until the relational framework is altered in the more adaptive way through practice (see committed action).

Therapists at our clinic work to help patients be more flexible when deciding whether a past, present, or future perspective is most adaptive for each situation as it arises. For example, choosing to drink alcohol after work each day may have helped manage stress in the past, but it also raises the possibility of PG as discipline slips with alcohol intake. By developing a present moment focus and using mindfulness techniques, healthy adaptive ways to manage stress in the key moments after work can be encouraged as a genuine alternative to the automatic process of drinking and the subsequent engagement in PG.

Defining Valued Directions Defining values involves stepping back from day-to-day life to examine the greater possibilities that support the reasons patients have for being and their struggles. A key part of this process is to establish a framework for constructive action. Values are the response given to the question: 'In a world where you could choose to have your life be about something, what would you choose?' (Wilson and Murrell 2004, p135). In ACT, values are defined as verbally constructed, globally applied, desired, chosen life directions (Dahl et al. 2005). Again context remains important, so the concept of 'truth' implied in the values that are determined should be considered as helpful, or not, only in the particular situation at hand. In our clinic many PGs have responded well to the identification of their values as they provide a 'road map' for them to access in moving their lives in more adaptive directions. Although the values are never finally achieved, the mindful, aware, and intentional process of working towards them is fulfilling and is very helpful in behaviour change away from PG.

Committed Action Committed Action involves creating stronger patterns of effective behaviour that move an individual closer to their chosen values. This process shares many similarities with goal setting components of traditional behaviour therapies. As with the 'first wave' strategies, committed action in ACT sees goals as tangible objectives that can and should be met and reset over time. The settng of tangible goals also helps establish treatment as not just a 'once-off' theoretical exercise, and that it is not just limited to the time spent in the therapy sessions. In our clinic we say that this process is where the 'rubber hits the road' so that actual change is engaged in or the barriers preventing the changed behaviour are identified and altered. The committed action process involves a cycle of ongoing review, reset, and re-engagement.

Research on the Use of ACT for Problem Gamblers

The empirical evidence in support of ACT as an effective therapeutic technique continues to expand (see Ruiz 2012 for a review). The evidence currently supports the use of ACT as an effective treatment option for substance use disorders (Twohig et al. 2007). As substance use disorders share aetiological similarities with PG (Petry 2005), ACT appears to offer promise for treating certain PGs, yet only a small number of brief experimental-based ACT approaches have been tested with PGs to date. Like the substance use literature for ACT, the initial results for using ACT for PG appear to be promising.

In the first investigation of ACT in a gambling setting, Nastally and Dixon (2012) found that gamblers' irrational beliefs decreased after exposure to a brief ACT intervention delivered via computer. The design had a small number of gamblers complete a slot machine activity before and after the intervention, and then they were asked to rate how close each slot machine outcome was to a win (1 not at all close, 10 very close to a win). The intervention used a PowerPoint slide show explaining the ACT components, similar to the description above. Following the intervention, the gamblers' subjective ratings of near-miss outcomes decreased.

In an associated study, Whiting and Dixon (2014) evaluated acceptance and defusion strategies on gambling behaviour, delivered via an imaginal desensitisation task. The design had 30 gamblers randomly assigned to 30 imaginal desensitisation trials (either imagining slot machine gambling 30 times plus dropping quarters in a laundry machine three times or imagining dropping quarters in a laundry machine 30 times plus slot machine gambling three times). After the desensitisation task, the gamblers were asked to play on a slot machine for as long as they desired. Results showed that participants who had practised accepting gambling images and/or thoughts played less than participants who did not think about gambling images and/or thoughts.

The potential neurological impact of ACT was examined recently in college-aged PGs (Dixon et al. 2016). A randomised control design required 18 participants to complete two functional magnetic resonance imaging scans whilst the PGs imagined completing a slot machine activity. After the initial scan, 10 subjects were exposed to a total of 8 h of ACT delivered individually by a therapist, and the other 8 received no treatment. Using a mixed two-group (ACT, control), two-condition (wins, losses), and two-timeframe (pre, post) design, the self-report and behavioural aspects of the slot machine activity and the brain activation data were compared across time. Results indicated that at post-treatment, PGs in the ACT group reported higher rates of psychological flexibility and mindfulness than control gamblers. The brain activation patterns also differed significantly between groups for winning outcomes when compared to losing outcomes following treatment, in favour of those who received the treatment. These data suggest that psychological reconditioning of behavioural and neurological responses to various addictive stimuli are possible using ACT.

Dixon et al. (2016) commented that a successfully implemented ACT-based treatment for PGs could potentially make gambling less appetitive by disrupting existing relational networks between stimuli or by producing new competing relational frames that are in contrast to prior held frames. For example, patients exposed to a therapeutic intervention which alters relations targeted at larger value systems (e.g. if I gamble, then no bills get paid and gambling is the same as missing family time), then the patient might reduce gambling because those relational frames contain more aversive stimulus functions than before (Barnes-Holmes et al. 2004).

Whilst the above studies demonstrate some positive initial steps in using ACT for PG, the preliminary nature of the designs, methods used for detecting change, and low power of the studies means that the evidence-base for treatment use must be considered 'experimental' at this time. It is our anecdotal experience that some PG treatment practitioners draw comparisons between ACT and CBT interventions, suggesting that there is little difference in the practical application of these interventions. However, the differences in our practice of ACT and CBT are noteworthy, and the different emphasis appears to be favoured by certain clients who prefer acceptance-based over challenge-based interventions. In most cases the interventions are complementary, and the acceptance-based approaches appear to have good general acceptability in relapse prevention phases of treatment for PGs.

Case Study

A number of ACT interventions that we have used in the treatment of PGs are discussed below using the case study of a patient called Mark.

Mark was a 45-year-old accountant, who was diagnosed with a major depressive disorder 10 years prior to presenting to our clinic. Mark had been married for 20 years, had two children at high school, and previously owned a small accounting firm. He began gambling on horses in his late teens as he started attending licenced premises. He had been gambling on EGMs over the previous 5 years at a level that had resulted in him losing his business. At assessment, he was working for another employer, had a poor relationship with his wife and children, and had symptoms consistent with depression (anhedonia, poor sleep, difficulty concentrating, weight increase). He reported that he had always been shy and that he had withdrawn socially since losing his business. He stated that 'I only feel remotely like myself when I'm in front of an EGM. At those times I don't feel weighted down'. He was gambling three times per week and spending the majority of the money he could access. Self-exclusion and past cognitive-focused treatment had been unsuccessful.

As indicated above, ACT aims to develop 'psychological flexibility' rather than target symptom reduction. Mark was able to identify 'events', or urges, that preceded his gambling episodes. In the first session Mark was asked to describe his urges in terms of specific thoughts, emotions, and physical sensations. He was also asked to describe triggers that preceded the urges, and he was encouraged to identify urges in very descriptive terms to outline any associated images or memories. Mark reported that he felt anxious, 'keyed up', and light-headed and had some tingling in his stomach, sweating palms, and thoughts that he 'must be due a decent payout', 'I'll feel ten feet tall if I walk through the door at home and have some money to show them', and 'I have no other way of breaking through this debt, I'm a failure'. His emotions cycled between excitement, anger, fear, and hopelessness. He also reported being able to hear the sounds of his favourite EGM.

The first intervention using ACT began following the assessment and PG-related psychoeducation (see Chap. 2) and utilised strategies from the acceptance and cognitive defusion core processes. The goal was to help Mark see the urges in a new way, namely, as electrical impulses in his brain and body, and the historical maladaptive PG responses to the impulses were held in place by his own language and frames about himself and societal views of PGs. The therapist helped Mark to willingly accept the urges as described above and educated Mark about defusion so that he didn't try to experientially avoid the distress of the urges. The focus was on highlighting the unworkable strategies being used by Mark not any deficits in him as a person.

Mindful breathing techniques were used to allow Mark to notice the thoughts and emotions that were circling within him. Mark related well to the analogy of engaging in a championship wrestling match versus observing an uninteresting, non-provocative television commercial (Louma et al. 2007). It was put to Mark that if he relied on experiential avoidance in the current case, it would highly likely lead to and continue to maintain PG as a short-term strategy to reduce the distress associated with the urges, thus reinforcing the relational network. For homework, Mark was asked to spend time each day devoted to imagining his thoughts as being written on a karaoke screen with a bouncing ball on top of them, so the thoughts could be seen merely as language passing through his consciousness.

During the next phase of treatment, Mark was introduced to a mindfulness technique, to promote a greater level of focus on the present moment. It is our experience that in this phase of treatment that many clients report an understanding of mindfulness that includes the goal of 'clearing your mind of everything', which we describe as being closer to mindlessness than mindfulness. Mindfulness in the ACT treatment context involves increasing the awareness of what the internal and external experience is at the current point in time, and to recognise the 'pull' to either the past or future. In our clinic, therapists help patients learn this skill for better decision-making and behavioural repertoire expansion beyond automatic PG behaviours. One example of an experiential exercise involved Mark mindfully eating a sultana. This required him to slowly chew the sultana whilst noting the texture, weight, and flavour. Mark was told that when thoughts arose that took his focus from the sultana, he was to try and note the distracting thoughts and then reengage in focusing on the sultana eating experience, without criticism of himself. The session debrief focused on Mark drawing parallels to the language he used to describe his thoughts in the sultana exercise and when he was having urges, as well as the level of detail and enjoyment he experienced eating the sultana in the experiment compared to any other time he could remember. The therapist discussed how he may be able to start to accept the urge related thoughts, as he did with the intrusions in the sultana exercise, rather than trying to ignore or overly engage with them. Homework involved nominating times during the day that he was to deliberately activate his five senses to notice the present moment and to try and practise accepting whatever was detected in those times.

As Mark's mindfulness practice developed, the therapist introduced the concept of self as context, as described above. The previous mindfulness exercises were used to demonstrate that there were two distinct entities involved when being mindful: (1) the internal experience that was observed and (2) the 'self' that did the observing. The aim was to help Mark realise that no internal experience is inherently dangerous, controlling, or threatening and that his ability to control his internal state may be merely an illusion created by the use of problem solving language that is so effective in the external world. The therapist explained to Mark that understanding self as context meant that whilst his relational frame (1 above) was likely to provide information, it is distinct from his 'self' (2 above), and that learning to access both perspectives in situations was the goal.

The next sessions moved the focus of treatment to Mark's values. Mark was taken through the Values Compass exercise (Eifert and Forsyth 2005) to help distil his values and his surrent resource allocation to each of them. For homework Mark was asked to write the speech for his 80th birthday party as would be written by his wife. He was told to write it as if he had lived a value-based life. This exercise identified reliability, knowledge, and service to others as key values that were present at times when he had felt most satisfied in life. A discussion was then initiated in which the therapist and Mark agreed how his limited resources of time, attention, and energy were currently organised in service of the values he had just stated. The outcome was to develop committed actions to re-balance the pursuit of his values.

The final phase of the core ACT treatment was devoted to reviewing the previous content of sessions and tying key components together with associated 'committed action'. The focus was on establishing goals that were consistent with Mark's values. Mark set the goal of going for a 15-min walk each lunchtime and after work before he commenced his journey home for the next month and then review whether he would change that activity to keep him engaged. He also set the goals of practicing techniques from past sessions on alternate days for 1 month, as well as tightening his stimulus control measures around access to money. We agreed that the next round of goals would be for him to offer his services informally as a mentor to one of his work colleagues and that he would schedule 30 min a week into his calendar to review updates on tax management from the professional body for accountants. Appropriate clarity was created around these goals so they could be measured, and reality testing was done to ensure they were reasonable and achieveable. A follow-up session was organised, where goal-setting review was placed as agenda item 1. Relapse prevention strategies involved deepening the skills discussed above.

References

Barnes-Holmes, Y., Barnes-Holmes, D., McHugh, L., & Hayes, S. C. (2004). Relational frame theory: Some implications for understanding and treating human psychopathology. *International Journal of Psychology and Psychological Therapy, 4*(2), 355–375.

Dahl, J. C., Wilson, K. G., Luciano, C., & Hayes, S. C. (2005). *Acceptance and commitment therapy for chronic pain*. Reno: Colorado Press.

Dixon, M. R., Wilson, A. N., & Habib, R. (2016). Neurological evidence of acceptance and commitment therapy effectiveness in college-age gamblers. *Journal of Contextual Behavioral Science, 5*(2), 80–88.

Eifert, G., & Forsyth, J. (2005). *Acceptance and commitment therapy for anxiety disorders*. Oakland: New Harbinger Publications.

Harris, R. (2006). Embracing your demons: An overview of acceptance and commitment therapy. *Psychotherapy in Australia, 12*(4), 2–8.

Hayes, S. C., Strosahl, K. D., & Wilson, K. G. (1999). *Acceptance and commitment therapy: An experiential approach to behavior change*. New York: New Guildford Press.

Hayes, S. C., Barnes-Holmes, D., & Roche, B. (2001). *Relational frame theory: A post- Skinnerian account of human language and cognition*. New York: Plenum.

Hayes, S. C., & Strosahl, K. D. (2005). *A practical guide to acceptance and commitment therapy*. New York: Springer.

Hayes, S. C., Strosahl, K. D., Luoma, J., Smith, A. S., & Wilson, K. G. (2005). ACT case formulation. In H. S.C. & S. K.D. (Eds.), *Acceptance and commitment therapy: A practical clinical guide*. New York: Kluwer/Plenum.

Louma, J. B., Hayes, S. C., & Walser, R. D. (2007). Learning ACT: *An acceptance & commitment therapy skills-training manual for therapists*. Oakland: New Harbinger Publications.

Nastally, B. L., & Dixon, M. R. (2012). The effect of a brief acceptance and commitment therapy intervention on the near miss effect in problem gamblers. *The Psychological Record, 62*(4), 677–690.

Petry, N. M. (2005). *Pathological gambling: Etiology, comorbidity, and treatment*. Washington, DC: American Psychological Association.

Ruiz, F. J. (2012). Acceptance and commitment therapy versus traditional cognitive behavioural therapy: A systematic review and meta-analysis of current empirical evidence. *International Journal of Psychology and Psychological Therapy, 12*, 333–357.

Twohig, M. P., Shoenberger, D., & Hayes, S. C. (2007). A preliminary investigation of acceptance and commitment therapy as a treatment for marijuana dependence in adults. *Journal of Applied Behavior Analysis, 40*, 619–632. doi:10.1901/aba.2007.619-632.

Whiting, S. W., & Dixon, M. R. (2015). Examining contextual control in roulette gambling. *Journal of Applied Behavior Analysis, 48*(1), 204–208.

Wilson, K. G., & Murrell, A. (2004). Values work in acceptance and commitment therapy: Setting a course for behavioural treatment. In S. C. Hayes, V. M. Follette, & M. M. Linehan (Eds.), *Mindfulness and acceptance: Expanding the cognitive-behavioural tradition* (pp. 120–151). New York: Guildford Press.

Chapter 8
Dialectical Behaviour Therapy and Pathological Gambling

Kate Fennessy

Description of the Intervention

Dialectical behaviour therapy (DBT) was developed in the late 1980s by Marsha M. Linehan, a psychology researcher at the University of Washington (Linehan 1987). The therapy was designed to treat people with multiple problems and chronic suicidality, including those with a diagnosis of borderline personality disorder (BPD), a pervasive and persistent disorder involving emotional dysregulation, impulsivity, identity disturbance, problematic interpersonal relationships and suicidal or self-harm behaviours (American Psychiatric Association 2013, 5th ed.; Linehan 1993).

DBT is based on a biosocial understanding of the aetiology of BPD (Linehan 1987, 1993): an interaction of biological vulnerabilities with emotion regulation difficulties during stressful situations (Crowell et al. 2009; Linehan 1987, 1993; Linehan et al. 1991). The theory describes a biologically based disposition towards emotion vulnerability (Linehan 1993) on three separate axes: a relatively low threshold for responding to emotional stimuli, relatively intense emotional responses, and a relatively slow return to baseline level of emotional arousal. Vulnerabilities in attachment or trauma can cause individuals with this genetic loading to have difficulty learning how to cope with intense emotional reactions, are often invalidated and may be shaped to respond in escalating ways in order to get their needs met, such as by engaging in acts of self-harm.

Linehan observed burnout in therapists working with non-motivated and chronically suicidal patients who did not have good treatment engagement or positive outcomes and introduced the need for a commensurate commitment from patients in order to access the treatment. She noted that these patients commonly described being raised in profoundly invalidating environments and required a climate of

K. Fennessy (✉)
Gambling Treatment Program, St Vincents Hospital Sydney, Darlinghurst, NSW, Australia
e-mail: kate.fennessy@svha.org.au

C. McIntosh, K. O'Neill, *Evidence-Based Treatments for Problem Gambling*, SpringerBriefs in Psychology, DOI 10.1007/978-3-319-62485-3_8

particular warmth and kindness in which to develop a successful therapeutic alliance. As a result of this insight, DBT incorporates interventions designed to convey acceptance of the patient and to help the patient practise self-acceptance skills, in balance with change-oriented strategies. The outcome of Linehan's work is a comprehensive, evidence-based, cognitive behavioural treatment for BPD (Linehan 1993).

Key Tenets

DBT combines standard Western cognitive behavioural techniques for emotion regulation and reality testing with concepts of distress tolerance, acceptance and mindful awareness derived from Eastern meditative traditions. The therapy also draws from behavioural psychology, particularly applied behaviour analysis, as it incorporates behavioural analysis, exposure, contingency management, problem solving and stimulus control. DBT is based on the core conditions of balancing acceptance and change through the principle of dialectics, in which thesis and antithesis are synthesised. Therapists highlight both aspects of the dialectic (two apparently connected opposites), and the client develops an understanding that awareness of these opposites affords the possibility of change as they learn to better respond to their environment, fostering successive resolutions at increasingly more functional levels (Linehan 1987). DBT is also characterised by its adherence to a prescribed treatment structure, as well as its biosocial theory, five functions of treatment, dialectical philosophy, focus on emotion and relationships and descriptions of acceptance and mindfulness skills which are distinct from other third wave therapies.

Functions and Processes of Treatment

The five functions of DBT treatment include enhancing and generalising client capabilities, improving motivation, reducing dysfunctional behaviour, enhancing and maintaining therapist capabilities and motivation and structuring the environment. The core of the treatment rests in the client's development of the four key processes of DBT: mindfulness (being aware of the present moment, non-judgmentally), distress tolerance (coping with painful feelings by building resilience to reduce the impact of upsetting events), emotion regulation (managing challenging emotions without becoming overwhelmed or reacting in damaging and destructive ways) and interpersonal effectiveness (expressing personal needs and beliefs whilst protecting important relationships and treating others with respect; MacKay et al. 2007) . Mindfulness is understood to be the core competency underpinning the other three factors. These are designed to complement and treat the four core aspects of personality disorder: identity disturbance, affective instability, behavioural dysregulation and disturbed relatedness or negative relationships (Linehan 1987). DBT therefore aims to improve emotional coping across a number of life domains and thereby reducing the likelihood of engaging in destructive behaviours.

Treatment Structure

DBT involves four components: individual therapy, group skills training, a therapist consultation team which serves to support the therapist in providing the treatment and phone coaching, designed to help the patient generalise skills into their daily life. Original protocols delineate a 1-year enrolment in DBT, with weekly individual therapy sessions (1 h), skills group (1.5–2.5 h) and fortnightly therapist consultation team meeting (1–2 h). This original model of DBT has the strongest empirical backing; however, modified iterations of DBT are frequently delivered in modern clinical practice, for which the evidence is emerging.

Evidence Base

Clinically, DBT is frequently applied for multiproblematic patients in general, including those patients with comorbid Axis I and II disorders and who are suicidal or self-injurious. The efficacy of DBT has been demonstrated in well-controlled, randomised clinical trials in the treatment of borderline personality disorder (BPD), mood disorders, comorbid BPD and substance use problems, binge eating and other recurrent harmful behaviours and in the treatment of sexual abuse survivors (see Chapman 2006 for a review).

The 2002 Cochrane review of randomised controlled trials of psychological therapies for BPD suggested that although DBT was no better than treatment as usual (TAU) on some indices, it was shown as having consistently led to improved outcomes on reducing self-harm and parasuicidal behaviour and suicidal ideation (Binks et.al 2006, see also Linehan et al. 1999, 2006; Carter et al. 2010; Turner 2000; Linehan et al. 1991, 2006; McMain et al. 2009), particularly for more severely affected BPD patients (Verheul et al. 2003). These results have also been replicated for patients with a cluster B or other personality diagnoses (e.g. Priebe et al. 2012). Some positive outcomes have been shown to be equivalent between DBT and general psychiatric treatment (McMain et al. 2009), transference-focused psychotherapy (Clarkin et al. 2007), collaborative management of suicidality (Andreasson et al. 2016) or TAU (Carter et al. 2010). Linehan et al. (2006) found that medical risk, frequency of emergency department visits and psychiatric hospitalisations were significantly reduced for BPD patients receiving DBT when compared to other therapies delivered by expert clinicians.

Studies on comorbid BPD and drug dependence have found DBT to have improved outcomes compared to TAU (Linehan et al. 1999) and, when compared to other treatments involving validation, was as effective at reducing drug use, however was less effective at maintaining participants in treatment (Linehan et al. 2002). DBT has been shown to effectively reduce frequency of alcohol intake as well as improve global mental health functioning of patients with BPD (Binks et al. 2006). DBT has also been shown to improve behavioural and attitudinal features associated with concurrent disordered eating and substance use for patients that do not have a diagnosis of personality disorder (Courbasson et al. 2012). In terms of processes, results suggest that all four of the DBT modules are the mechanisms responsible for subsequent positive behavioural and psychological change and improved outcomes (Stepp et al. 2008; Axelrod et al. 2011). In addition, DBT has been found to improve features associated with BPD in other patient populations and with adaptations to the original structure (e.g. Koons et al. 2001; Lynch et al. 2007; Lynch et al. 2003), including emerging indications of its efficacy as a transdiagnostic treatment for emotion dysregulation (Neacsiu et al. 2014).

The Use of DBT in the Treatment of Pathological Gambling

Uses in the Literature

While some findings indicate reductions in gambling during treatment for BPD (e.g. Verheul et al. 2003), only a handful of reported studies were found to have used DBT as a treatment for PG. Most recently, Christensen et al. (2013) trialled the use of a brief 9-week DBT group program for 14 treatment-resistant pathological gamblers (PGs) in Melbourne, Australia. They found statistically and clinically significant improvements in self-reported psychological distress, mindfulness and distress tolerance skill use, and 83% were abstinent or reduced their gambling expenditure pre- to post-treatment. Statistically, however, there was no significant change in substance use, gambling behaviour or personal effectiveness. There was no control group and no follow-up measures were reported.

A small informal report by Querney (2006) recorded general improvements in eight patients with either a PG or substance use disorder in a 9-month modified DBT course. Although specific data was not published, findings included reported "excellent" scores in using skills and primary behaviour target outcomes, degree of emotion was also rated as predominantly "very good" and qualitative reports by participants were very positive. Lastly, Korman et al. (2005) randomly assigned 42 PGs with comorbid anger problems, half of whom also had substance use problems, to a 12-week DBT program or TAU condition. The latter group received individual CBT focusing on cognitions and relapse prevention. There were no differences between the groups at baseline. It was found that the modified DBT program group had better retention and reported significantly less gambling at 14 and 26 weeks post baseline, as well as reduced anger at 14 weeks post baseline. Both treatments did show significant reductions in both gambling and anger, whilst only the modified DBT treatment showed significantly reduced substance use.

It appears from these few examples that DBT has potential as a useful intervention for PGs, perhaps particularly for those who are less responsive to traditional CBT. This treatment resistance may be attributable to personality traits or comorbidities affecting engagement and responsivity. It is of note and encouraging that moderate effect sizes were found even with the relatively brief interventions reported (Christensen et al. 2013).

Potential Uses in the Pathological Gambling Population

A high rate of overlap between PG and personality disorder is notable, particularly cluster B traits (Fernandez- Montalvo and Echeburua 2004; Bagby et al. 2008; Blaszczynski and Steel 1998). A meta-analysis conducted by Dowling et al. (2015) found that almost half (47.9%) of PGs displayed comorbid personality disorder, again with primarily cluster B features (17.6%). A more recent study of 168 treatment-seeking PGs in Australia found similar prevalence rates (Brown et al. 2016). These findings are also indicative of similarities between the two groups across the biosocial developmental model of BPD (Brown et al. 2015).

A number of other psychiatric disorders have been shown to co-occur with PG (Petry 2005; Crockford and El-Guebaly 1998; Lorains et al. 2011), and the association between PG and BPD extends to common comorbidities, which frequently form the behavioural targets for DBT treatment. These include substance use disorders (Cowlishaw et al. 2014; Petry 2007; Trull et al. 2000; Kim et al. 2006; Ste-Marie et al. 2006), suicidality and incidence of suicide attempts (Black et al. 2004; MacCallum and Blascyszcki 2003), depression (Stanley and Wilson 2006), emotional difficulties (Jacob et al. 2008; Kaare et al. 2009; Korman et al. 2005; Williams et al. 2011), dissociative symptoms (Berk et al. 2007; Delfabbro et al. 2006; Wanner et al. 2006), impulsivity (Linehan 1993; Nower and Blaszczynski 2006) and social and relationship issues and interpersonal conflict (Bouchard et al. 2009; Bray et al. 2007; Korman et al. 2005, 2008). This high symptom overlap can inform future treatment directions for PG populations by considering treatments shown to be effective for comorbid personality disorder and other commonly co-occurring conditions, such as DBT. Despite the high comorbidity of PG with other psychiatric disorders, there is little evidence on which to base treatment recommendations for these comorbid groups (Dowling et al. 2016).

The concept of emotion regulation is featured in many models of psychopathology, and it has been proposed that individuals with poorly regulated emotions may more frequently engage in maladaptive behaviours such as gambling, in order to escape from, or to downregulate their emotions. Indications of deficits in emotion regulation in PGs may signify a need to consider these underlying vulnerabilities in addition to directly targeting gambling behaviours in treatment (Williams et al.

2011). De Lisle et al. (2014) also identified emotional dysregulation as a mediator of the mechanism of PG in relation to psychological distress, as well as dispositional mindfulness as a mediator of gambling severity, amongst other factors (de Lisle et al. 2012). Models of the cognitive mechanisms underlying PG behaviour suggest an inverse relationship between mindfulness and gambling severity, with treatment-seeking PGs displaying significantly lower scores on measures of mindfulness than control groups (de Lisle et al. 2014). This is suggestive of the applicability of mindfulness training and mindfulness-based therapies such as DBT, as an avenue to improve efficacy of existing treatment.

Qualitative Review

When examining areas of comorbidity mentioned in this chapter, including difficulties in relationships, suicidality, emotional dysregulation and mediators of gambling severity identified as low mindfulness and low emotion regulation skills, the implications for DBT as an appropriate treatment for PG appear theoretically strong. This is particularly the case in the domains of attention to the therapeutic alliance, client motivations, and therapeutic boundaries, given its efficacy in the treatment of other addictions and problem behaviour. Process research is needed to delineate which modules are effective for subgroups of the PG population-seeking treatment, due to parallels with other available treatments. Despite similarities in models of psychopathology between BPD and PG, and the treatment success of DBT as a treatment for the former group, there has been very little evidence for its application within the PG population, and the limited available literature has severe methodological limitations. Modified and shorter applications of the therapy appear to show moderate effects even with smaller groups, and the ability for DBT to assist various patient groups to regulate their affect is a promising outcome for PGs who gamble to fulfil this function. The evidence suggests a cautiously hopeful outlook for the use of this intervention for a subgroup of PGs who may not benefit as strongly in TAU, in particular those patients with comorbid personality features affecting mood and/or substance use disorders.

Case Study

Suzie is a 35-year-old woman who has engaged in daily gambling on electronic gaming machines over the past 5 years. Suzie lives alone with her parents, grandmother and older brother, and she works as a freelance chartered accountant. She describes her parents as "the best parents in the world" but also noted that she feels distant from them and closest to her brother. Suzie is otherwise socially isolated and describes chronic thoughts of suicidality, low mood and distress. She presented to an outpatient specialist service for individual treatment for PG after her family discovered her lying to each of them about why she needed to borrow money.

Suzie described always feeling "empty" and noted that she would cut her arms and stomach during times of distress from age 18 to 28, commencing around the time she finished high school. Suzie also reported a period of heavy alcohol use from age 26 to 28, where she would frequently "drink to blackout", and she now no longer drinks alcohol as a result. She reported one significant romantic relationship which lasted for 10 years from age 21, describing her ex-partner as "cold" and "a user", and that she often felt suicidal when she believed he was withholding affection or attention. Suzie had started gambling alone at a local pub at age 30, and at age 31, in the context of the break-up of her relationship, her gambling became more consuming and she looked for work less and less. She took to attending the pub throughout the day when it was quiet and avoided social contact. On assessment, Suzie presented as emotionally detached, but at other times would become enraged when she could not reach her therapist immediately via phone and rescheduled her initial appointment three times prior to presentation. Suzie had commenced treatment on two prior occasions but had been unable to sustain her attendance. On assessment, her symptoms met diagnostic criteria for major depression, PG, and BPD traits. She reported that her gambling was the biggest problem in her life at the moment as it was causing her to feel low, created problems in her family relationships, and was getting in the way of her goals. She identified that gambling had an emotionally "numbing" effect and assisted her to avoid difficult situations or affect. Suzie felt motivated to engage in treatment in order to improve her relationships, however was ambivalent about abstinence.

Suzie engaged in individual therapy, comprised of orientation, risk management, motivational interviewing, stimulus control, behavioural analysis, contingency management and problem-solving strategies to control her gambling. Psychoeducation about gambling, the biosocial model and a shared formulation were developed, and emotion regulation strategies introduced. After three individual sessions, Suzie agreed to concurrent referral to a hospital-based 12-week DBT course. The shared rationale for DBT was to assist Suzie to develop distress tolerance and emotion regulation skills, assisting her to reduce her arousal in order to choose alternative and more value consistent actions. Suzie engaged well and was able to attend and remain in the group and was supported to repeat the course the following year. Suzie attended 25 individual therapy sessions on a fortnightly basis and 21 group DBT sessions. At discharge, she had practised abstinence for 6 months with no emergent maladaptive coping strategies reported and was engaging in emotion regulation skill practice regularly. She reported occasional suicidal thoughts in response to anxiety relating to online dating. She was referred to a private practitioner specialising in attachment trauma and followed up 3 months later via phone. At this time, Suzie reported having remained abstinent from gambling, alcohol use or parasuicidal behaviour and was enjoying regular boxing class and social outlets relating to her gym. She was seeing her family each week and was paying back her debt slowly. Suzie attributed a more stable mood and increased self-efficacy and self-esteem to having overcome her gambling problem.

References

American Psychiatric Association. (2013). *Diagnostic and statistical manual of mental disorders* (5th ed.). Arlington: American Psychiatric Publishing.

Andreasson, K., Krogh, J., Wenneberg, C., Jessen, H., Krakauer, K., Gluud, C., Thomsen, R. R., Randers, L., & Nordentoft, M. (2016). Effectiveness of dialectical behavior therapy versus collaborative assessment and management of suicidality treatment for reduction of self-harm in adults with borderline personality traits and disorder- a randomized observer-blinded clinical trial. *Journal of Depression and Anxiety, 33*, 520–530.

Axelrod, S. R., Perepletchikova, F., Holtzman, K., & Sinha, R. (2011). Emotion regulation and substance use frequency in women with substance dependence and borderline personality disorder receiving dialectical behaviour therapy. *The American Journal of Drug and Alcohol Abuse, 37*, 37–42.

Bagby, M., Bachon, D. D., Bulmash, E., & Quilty, L. C. (2008). Personality disorders and pathological gambling: A review and re-examination of prevalence rates. *Journal of Personality Disorders, 22*, 191–207.

Berk, M. S., Jeglic, E., Brown, G. K., Henriques, G. R., & Beck, A. T. (2007). Characteristics of recent suicide attempts with and without borderline personality. *Archives of Suicide Research, 11*, 91–104.

Binks, C., Fenton, M., McCarthy, L., Lee, T., Adams, C. E., & Duggan, C. (2006). *Psychological therapies for people with borderline personality disorder*. Cochrane Database of Systematic Reviews: John Wiley & Sons.

Black, D. W., Blum, N., Pfohl, B., & Hale, N. (2004). Suicidal behaviour in borderline personality disorder: Prevalence, risk factors, prediction, and prevention. *Journal of Personality Disorders, 18*, 226–239.

Blaszczynski, A., & Steel, Z. (1998). Personality disorders among pathological gamblers. *Journal of Gambling Studies, 14*(1), 51–71.

Bouchard, S., Sabourin, S., Lussier, Y., & Villeneuve, E. (2009). Relationship quality and stability in couples where one partner suffers from borderline personality disorder. *Journal of Marital and Family Therapy, 35*, 446–455.

Bray, S., Barrowclough, C., & Lobban, F. (2007). The social problem-solving abilities of people with borderline personality disorder. *Behaviour Research and Therapy, 45*, 1419–1417.

Brown, M., Allen, J. S., & Dowling, N. A. (2015). The application of an etiological model of personality disorders to problem gambling. *Journal of Gambling Studies, 31*, 1179. doi:10.1007/s10899-014-9504-z.

Brown, M., Oldenhof, E., Allen, J. S., & Dowling, N. A. (2016). An empirical study of personality disorders among treatment-seeking problem gamblers. *Journal of Gambling Studies, 32*(4), 1079–1100. Online publication date: 26-Mar-2016.

Carter, G. L., Willcox, C. H., Lewin, T. J., Conrad, A. M., & Bendit, N. (2010). Hunter DBT project: Randomized controlled trial of dialectical behaviour therapy in women with borderline personality disorder. *Australian New Zealand Journal of Psychiatry, 44*, 162–173.

Chapman, A. L. (2006). Dialectical behavior therapy: Current indications and unique elements. *Psychiatry (Edgmont), 3*(9), 62–68.

Christensen, D. R., Dowling, N. A., Jackson, A. C., Brown, M., Russo, J., Francis, K. L., & Umemoto, A. (2013). A proof of concept for using brief dialectical behavior therapy as a treatment for problem gambling. *Behaviour Change, 30*(2), 117–137. doi:10.1017/bec.2013.10.

Clarkin, J. F., Levy, K. N., Lenzenweger, M. F., & Kernberg, O. F. (2007). Evaluating three treatments for borderline personality disorder: A multiwave study. *American Journal of Psychiatry, 164*(6), 922–928.

Courbasson, C., Nishikawa, Y., & Dixon, L. (2012). Outcome of dialectical behaviour therapy for concurrent eating and substance use disorders. *Clinical Psychology and Psychotherapy, 19*(5), 434–449.

Cowlishaw, S., Merkouris, S., Chapman, A., & Radermacher, H. (2014). Pathological and problem gambling in substance use treatment: A systematic review and meta-analysis. *Journal of Substance Abuse Treatment, 46*(2), 98.

Crockford, D. N., & el-Guebaly, N. (1998). Psychiatric co-morbidity in pathological gambling: A critical review. *Canadian Journal of Psychiatry, 43*, 43–50.

Crowell, S. E., Beauchaine, T. P., & Linehan, M. M. (2009). A biosocial development model borderline personality: Elaborating and extending Linehan's theory. *Psychological Bulletin, 135*, 45–510.

de Lisle, S., Dowling, N. A., & Allen, S. J. (2012). Mindfulness and problem gambling: A review of the literature. *Journal of Gambling Studies, 28*, 719–739.

de Lisle, S., Dowling, N. A., & Allen, J. S. (2014). Mechanisms of action in the relationship between mindfulness and problem gambling behaviour. *International Journal of Mental Health Addiction, 12*, 206. doi:10.1007/s11469-014-9475-4.

Delfabbro, P., Lahn, J., & Grabosky, P. (2006). Psychosocial correlates of problem gambling in Australian students. *Australian and New Zealand Journal of Psychiatry, 40*, 587–595.

Dowling, N. A., Cowlishaw, S., Jackson, A. C., Merkouris, S. S., Francis, K. L., et al. (2015). The prevalence of comorbid personality disorders in treatment-seeking problem gamblers: A systematic review and meta-analysis. *Journal of Personality Disorders, 29*(6), 735–754. doi:10.1521/pedi_2014_28_168.

Dowling, N. A., Merkouris, S. S., & Lorains, F. K. (2016). Interventions for comorbid problem gambling and psychiatric disorders: Advancing a developing field of research. *Addictive Behaviours, 58*, 21–30.

Fernandez- Montalvo, J., & Echeburua, E. (2004). Pathological gambling and personality disorders: An exploratory study with the IPDE. *Journal of Personality Disorders, 18*, 500–505.

Jacob, G. A., Guenzler, C., Zimmermann, S., Scheel, C. N., Rusch, N., et al. (2008). Time course of anger and other emotions in women with borderline personality disorder: A preliminary study. *Journal of Behaviour Therapy and Experimental Psychiatry, 39*, 391–402.

Kaare, P., Mottus, R., & Konstabel, K. (2009). Pathological gambling in Estonia: Relationships with personality, self-esteem, emotional states and cognitive ability. *Journal of Gambling Studies, 25*, 377–390.

Kim, S. W., Grant, J. E., Eckert, E. D., Faris, P. L., & Hartman, B. K. (2006). Pathological gambling and mood disorders: Clinical associations and treatment implications. *Journal of Affective Disorders, 92*, 109–116.

Koons, C. R., Robins, C. J., Tweed, J. L., Lynch, T. R., Gonzelez, A. M., Morse, J. Q., et al. (2001). Efficacy of dialectical behaviour therapy in women veterans with borderline personality disorder. *Behavior Therapy, 32*, 371–390.

Korman, L., Collins, J., Littman-Sharp, N., McMain, S., & Skinner, W. (2005). *Concurrent gambling, substance use and anger: Development of a brief integrated treatment (final report)*. Guelph: Ontario Problem Gambling Research Centre.

Korman, L., Collins, J., Dutton, D., Dhayananthan, B., Littman-Sharp, N., & Skinner, W. (2008). Problem gambling and intimate partner violence. *Journal of Gambling Studies, 24*, 13–23.

Linehan, M. M. (1987). Dialectical behavioral therapy: A cognitive behavioral appraoch to parasuicide. *Journal of Personality Disorders, 1*, 328–333.

Linehan, M. M. (1993). *Cognitive-behavioral treatment of borderline personality disorder*. New York: Guilford Press.

Linehan, M. M., Armstrong, H. E., Suarez, A., Allmon, D., & Heard, H. L. (1991). Cognitive-behavioural treatment of chronically suicidal borderline patients. *Archives of General Psychiatry, 48*, 1060–1064.

Linehan, M. M., Schmidt, H., Dimeff, L. A., Craft, C. C., Kanter, M. A., & Comtois, K. A. (1999). Dialectical behavior therapy for patients with borderline personality disorder and drug-dependence. *The American Journal on Addictions, 8*(4), 279–292.

Linehan, M. M., Dimeff, L. A., Reynolds, S. K., Comtois, K. A., Welch, S. S., Heagerty, P., & Kivlahan, D. R. (2002). Dialectical behavior therapy versus comprehensive validation therapy plus 12-step for the treatment of opioid dependent women meeting criteria for borderline personality disorder. *Drug and Alcohol Dependence, 67*(1), 13–26.

Linehan, M. M., Comtois, K. A., Murray, A. M., Brown, M. Z., Gallop, R. J., Heard, H. L., Korslund, K. E., Tutek, D. A., Reynolds, S. K., & Lindenboim, N. (2006). Two-year randomized controlled trial and follow-up of dialectical behaviour therapy vs. therapy by experts for suicidal behaviour and borderline personality disorder. *Archives of General Psychiatry, 63*, 757–766.

Lorains, F. K., Cowlishaw, S., & Tomas, S. (2011). Prevalence of co-morbid disorders in problem and pathological gambling. *Addiction, 106*, 490–498.

Lynch, T. R., Morse, J. Q., Mendelson, T., & Robins, C. J. (2003). Dialectical behavior therapy for depressed older adults. *American Journal of Geriatric Psychiatry, 11*, 33–45.

Lynch, T. R., Cheavens, J. S., Cukrowicz, K. C., Thorp, S. R., Bronner, L., & Beyer, J. (2007). Treatment of older adults with co-morbid personality disorder and depression: A dialectical behavior therapy approach. *International Journal of Geriatric Psychiatry, 22*(2), 131–143.

MacCallum, F., & Blaszczynski, A. (2003). Pathological gambling and suicidality: An analysis of severity and lethality. *Suicide and Life Threatening Behavior, 33*, 88–98.

MacKay, M., Wood, J. C., & Brantley, J. (2007). *Dialectical behaviour therapy skills workbook: Practical DBT exercises for learning mindfulness, interpersonal effectiveness, emotion regulation, & distress tolerance*. Oakland: New Harbinger Publications.

McMain, S. F., Links, P. A., Gnam, W. H., Guimond, T., Cardish, R. J., Korman, L., & Streiner, D. L. (2009). A randomized trial of dialectical behaviour therapy versus general psychiatric management for borderline personality disorder. *American Journal of Psychiatry, 166*, 1365–1374.

Neacsiu, A. D., Eberle, J. W., Kramer, R., Wiesmann, T., & Linehan, M. M. (2014). Dialectical behavior therapy skills for transdiagnostic emotion dysregulation: A pilot randomized controlled trial. *Behaviour Research and Therapy, 59*, 40–51.

Nower, L., & Blaszczynski, A. (2006). Impulsivity and pathological gambling: A descriptive model. *International Gambling Studies, 6*, 61–75.

Petry, N. M. (2005). *Pathological gambling: Etiology, comorbidity, and treatment*. Washington, DC: American Psychological Association.

Petry, N. M. (2007). Gambling and substance use disorders: Current status and future directions. *The American Journal on Addictions, 16*, 1–9.

Priebe, S., Bhatti, N., Barnicot, K., Bremner, S., Gaglia, A., Katsakou, C., Molosankwe, I., McCrone, P., & Zinkler, M. (2012). Effectiveness and cost-effectiveness of dialectical behaviour therapy for self-harming patients with personality disorder: A pragmatic randomised controlled trial. *Psychotherapy and Psychosomatics, 81*, 356–365.

Querney, D. (2006). STEPS: A modified DBT group for preventing relapse among problem gamblers and substance abusers. Retrieved March 25, 2017, from http://www.responsiblegambling.org/articles/deirdre_querney_discovery_2006.pdf

Stanley, B., & Wilson, S. T. (2006). Heightened subjective experience of depression in borderline personality disorder. *Journal of Personality Disorders, 20*, 307–318.

Ste-Marie, C., Gupta, R., & Derevensky, J. (2006). Anxiety and social stress related to adolescent gambling behaviour and substance use. *Journal of Child and Adolescent Substance Use, 15*, 55–74.

Stepp, S. D., Epler, A. J., Jahng, S., & Trull, T. J. (2008). The effect of dialectical behaviour therapy skills use on borderline personality disorder features. *Journal of Personality Disorders, 22*, 549–563.

Trull, T., Sher, K. J., Minks-Brown, C., Durbin, J., & Burr, R. (2000). Borderline personality disorder and substance use disorders: A review and integration. *Clinical Psychology Review, 20*, 235–253.

Turner, R. M. (2000). Naturalistic evaluation of dialectical behaviour therapy-oriented treatment for borderline personality disorder. *Cognitive and Behavioural Practice, 7*(4), 413–419.

Verheul, R., Van Den Bosch, L. M., Koeter, M. W., De Ridder, M. A., Stijnen, T., & Van Den Brink, W. (2003). Dialectical behaviour therapy for women with borderline personality disorder. *The British Journal of Psychiatry, 182*(2), 135–140.

Wanner, B., Ladoucer, R., Auclair, A. V., & Vitaro, F. (2006). Flow and dissociation: Examination of mean levels, cross links, and links to emotional well-being across sports and recreational and pathological gambling. *Journal of Gambling Studies, 22*, 289–304.

Williams, A. D., Grisham, J. R., Erskine, A., & Cassedy, E. (2011). Deficits in emotion regulation associated with pathological gambling. *British Journal of Clinical Psychology, 51*, 223–238. doi:10.1111/j.2044-8260.2011.02022.x.

Chapter 9
Pharmacological Management of Problem Gambling

Alison Bautovich

There is a reasonably robust body of research to support the use of psychobehavioural therapies in the treatment of problem gambling (PG). However, these therapies are often resource intensive, tend to rely on the motivation of the individual and may have limitations in terms of retention rates and durability of response (Bartley and Bloch 2013; Cowlishaw et al. 2012; Petry et al. 2006).

The use of pharmacological agents for the treatment of PG has largely grown from their development and use in substance use disorders (SUDs). Given the similarities in phenomenological and neurobiological aspects between PG and SUDs, PG is commonly conceptualised as a behavioural addiction as reflected in the recent change in classification of the disorder in DSM V (American Psychiatric Association 2013; Petry et al. 2014).

In broad terms, the pharmacological approaches utilised in PG have been to use medications that modulate reward mechanisms via alteration in the glutamatergic, serotonergic, dopaminergic and opioidergic transmission within mesolimbic circuits (Piquet-Pessoa and Fontenelle 2016).

The main classes of medications used in SUDs and PG are (i) opioid antagonists, (ii) selective serotonin reuptake inhibitors (SSRIs), (iii) mood stabilisers and (iv) glutamate antagonists:

(i) Opioid antagonists

The use of opioid antagonists in alcohol use disorder was largely based on preclinical studies that showed that dopamine release and self-administration of alcohol were diminished in animals given naltrexone (NTX) (Altshuler et al. 1980; Benjamin et al. 1993). Opioid receptors are widely distributed in the mesolimbic

A. Bautovich (✉)
Prince of Wales Hospital, School of Psychiatry, University of New South Wales, Sydney, NSW, Australia
e-mail: Alison.Bautovich@health.nsw.gov.au

C. McIntosh, K. O'Neill, *Evidence-Based Treatments for Problem Gambling*, SpringerBriefs in Psychology, DOI 10.1007/978-3-319-62485-3_9

system and have been implicated in the hedonic aspects of reward processing (Australian Medicines Handbook 2017). The use of opioid antagonists in addiction, particularly alcohol disorders, is thought to stem from their ability to disinhibit gamma-aminobutyric acid (GABA) input to dopamine neurons, thereby inhibiting dopamine release in the nucleus accumbens and ventral pallidum. This, in turn, is thought to result in diminished urges to engage in the addictive behaviours and longer periods of abstinence (Kim 1998). Naltrexone currently has approval for use in alcohol and/or opioid dependence.

Given their ability to modulate dopaminergic transmission in the mesolimbic circuitry, as well as the fact that treatment-seeking problem gamblers frequently have high rates of alcohol use and substance use disorders (Cowlishaw et al. 2014), this class of medications are the most well-studied and empirically supported pharmacological agents in the treatment of PG. Naltrexone, a mu, delta and kappa opioid receptor antagonist, is the most well studied of the opioid antagonists. Nalmefene, a mu and delta opioid antagonist and kappa partial agonist has also been studied; however its use has been mostly in European populations. To date, there have been six trials of regular naltrexone use in PG – one open-label trial and five double-blind placebo-controlled trials. There have also been two trials focused on as needed use of naltrexone.

In a recent meta-analysis conducted by Bartley and Bloch (2013), the five placebo-controlled trials of naltrexone versus placebo trials were analysed. A fixed effects meta-analysis demonstrated a small, but significant benefit compared to placebo (SMD 0.22±0.10 95% CI: 0.03–0.41), with no significant difference in effect size compared with placebo found between the two opioid antagonists studied. The authors commented on the significant amount of heterogeneity between trial results and the limited number of studies that utilised intention to treat analysis. Furthermore, they cautioned that the treatment effect of opioid antagonists found in the meta-analysis and earlier systematic reviews may be driven by a small number of flawed early trials of opiate antagonists.

There is a suggestion that the greater intensity of pretreatment gambling urges as well as a positive familial history of alcoholism may be associated with better treatment response to naltrexone (Grant et al. 2008) in those seeking treatment for PG.

(ii) SSRIs

Serotonin has several functions in the brain that are relevant to the field of substance use. Serotonin is important in the regulation of mood, arousal, cognition and impulsivity. Projections to the nucleus accumbens are also involved in controlling motivation to perform certain behaviours, including the abuse of alcohol and other drugs. Decreased serotonin function within the ventromedial prefrontal cortex is thought to contribute to disinhibition and pathological gambling. Together, these findings suggest that decreased serotonin function within the ventromedial prefrontal cortex may result in disinhibition and contribute to PG (Grant and Kim 2006).

The action of SSRIs is thought to be primarily due to reabsorption blockade, resulting in increased levels of serotonin in the synaptic cleft. As such, these agents are often considered in the treatment of substance use disorders and PG. Additionally, given that PG frequently co-occurs with mood and anxiety disorders (a recent meta-analysis of 11 population studies across 5 countries estimated the rates of mood disorders co-occurring with PG was 38% and anxiety disorders was 37% (van den Brink 2012)), it was hoped that anti-depressants, particularly the mostly well-tolerated SSRIs, may have an important role in the treatment of PG.

Unfortunately, most of the studies involving SSRIs have excluded subjects with a comorbid diagnosis of a mood or anxiety disorder. Furthermore, the results from studies looking at the efficacy of SSRIs in PG have been mixed, with most uncontrolled studies showing a positive effect, but almost all randomised controlled studies showing negative or non-significant effects (van den Brink 2012).

In a randomised controlled trial of sertraline (50–150 mg/day) in 60 patients, outcome data at 6 months did not demonstrate a significant difference between the sertraline and placebo groups (Saiz-Ruiz et al. 2005). Double-blind placebo-controlled trials of both fluvoxamine (Blanco et al. 2002; Hollander et al. 2000) and paroxetine (Grant et al. 2003; Kim et al. 2002) have shown conflicting results. There have been two open trials of escitalopram (Black et al. 2007; Grant and Potenza 2006), with one of the study populations being patients with PG comorbid with anxiety (Grant and Potenza 2006). Both studies reported improved gambling outcomes in those treated with escitalopram.

(iii) Mood stabilisers

Mood stabilisers have shown anti-impulsive properties as well as efficacy in reducing cravings and preventing relapse in different substance-related disorders (Di Nicola et al. 2014; Vornik and Brown 2006). Several authors, including Pallanti et al. (2002), have highlighted the similarities between PG and bipolar disorder. This, added to the fact that SSRIs may exacerbate gambling behaviours and mood symptoms in PGs with comorbid bipolar affective disorder (Labuzek et al. 2014), led researchers to seek alternative medications for this specific subgroup.

The investigation of mood stabilisers in the treatment of PG has primarily focused on lithium and sodium valproate. Lithium is a medication that has good evidence for the control of manic episodes as well as in the prevention of further mood episodes in bipolar affective disorder. The actions of lithium are not fully understood; however, inhibition of dopamine release and enhancement of serotonin release are two supposed actions that are relevant to the field of addiction (Australian Medicines Handbook 2017). There is only one double-blind placebo-controlled study examining the use of lithium in PG. This study of 40 patients with gambling and bipolar spectrum disorders (bipolar type II, bipolar not otherwise specified and cyclothymia) used sustained release lithium with a mean lithium level of 0.87 mEq/L. The study concluded that lithium was superior to placebo, both in terms of reducing gambling symptoms and improving affective instability during the 10 weeks of treatment (Hollander et al. 2005). Interestingly, a PET study examining cortical areas implicated in impulse control disorders found neuroimaging correlates for the efficacy of lithium in PGs with a further increase in relative glucose metabolic rates in these areas (Hollander et al. 2008).

Sodium valproate is a medication that is used in the treatment of epilepsy as well as in the treatment of acute and maintenance phases of bipolar affective disorder. Sodium valproate has multiple mechanisms of action; however, its ability to increase levels of GABA and inhibit glutamate is thought to account for its role in substance and behavioural addictions, as well as its mood stabilising properties (Australian Medicines Handbook 2017). The use of sodium valproate in PG is limited; however, a single blind study of lithium and valproate conducted on pathological gamblers without a comorbid diagnosis of bipolar affective disorder found both mood stabilisers to be effective (Pallanti et al. 2002).

(iv) Glutamate antagonists

There is a significant body of mostly preclinical evidence that suggests a critical role for glutamate transmission and glutamate receptors in drug reward, reinforcement and relapse (Grant and Chamberlain 2016). Additionally, glutamate seems to be involved in long-lasting neuroadaptation in the corticostriatal circuitry (Kalivas 2009). Glutamate has been shown to be involved in associative learning and can adversely affect communication between the prefrontal cortex and the nucleus accumbens resulting in reward-seeking behaviours (Kalivas and Volkow 2011).

The main agents studied in the substance use literature are topiramate, amantadine, memantine and N-acetylcysteine (NAC). Topiramate is a GABAergic and anti-glutamatergic medication that is primarily used in epilepsy. Topiramate has shown promise in several addiction-related disorders including binge eating disorder (Claudino et al. 2007) and alcohol dependence (Johnson et al. 2007). Specific to the field of PG, there has been one fairly small ($n = 20$ topiramate, $n = 22$ placebo) double-blind trial of topiramate in problem gambling (Berlin et al. 2013). Although no statistical significant differences were found between the two groups in the primary outcome measure (obsessions subscale of the Y-BOCS modified for PG), there was an observed trend in terms of decreased impulsivity in the treatment group. In a more recent study of topiramate combined with cognitive restructuring, topiramate was shown to be superior to placebo. However, unlike the Berlin et al. study (2013), topiramate was found to affect features specific to gambling addiction rather than associated phenomena such as impulsivity or depression.

Amantadine is a non-specific glutamate blocker that is used in the treatment of Parkinson's disease. It has also been shown to have actions on dopaminergic neurotransmission (Labuzek et al. 2014). In one double-blind placebo-controlled trial of 17 patients with Parkinson's disease, amantadine was shown to be effective in improving outcome measures related to gambling. However, these improvements were short-lived, with scores increasing in the 1-week washout period (Thomas et al. 2010).

Memantine is a medication used in the treatment of moderate to severe Alzheimer's disease. It exerts influence on the glutamatergic system via NMDA antagonist action. Memantine has also been shown to modulate frontal lobe function (van Wageningen et al. 2010). An open-label trial of memantine in 29 individuals with PG showed improvement in measures of gambling behaviour as well as some cognitive tasks at the end of 10 weeks (Grant et al. 2010).

N-Acetylcysteine (NAC) is primarily used in the treatment of paracetamol overdose; however, it has also been shown to have glutamate-modulating properties and has been suggested to restore glutamate concentrations in the nucleus accumbens

(Hemby et al. 2005). Again, the use of this agent in the treatment of PG is limited. There has been one study of 27 subjects with gambling disorder where NAC was given for a period of 8 weeks. Those that responded were then randomised to receive either an additional 6 weeks of NAC or placebo. Significant differences were found both in the open and double-blind phases of the trial (Grant et al. 2007).

Qualitative Review

As Grant et al. (2016) observes, the systematic study of treatment efficacy and tolerability is in its infancy. As such, making clear treatment recommendations is challenging. Currently, there are no medications that are approved for use in the treatment of behavioural addictions, including PG (Grant et al. 2016). Despite this, pharmacological agents are frequently used in the problem gambling population, perhaps, at least in part, reflecting the high rates of psychiatric comorbidity in this group.

The existing evidence base has several limitations. Given that many of the studies exclude subjects with comorbid psychiatric or substance use disorders and are made up of subjects requesting treatment, often in highly specialised treatment settings, the results may have limitations in their applicability to a broad range of individuals with PG. As suggested by Dowling et al. (2016), comorbidity is generally the rule, rather than the exception; thus, studies investigating the efficacy of treatment interventions in PG need to measure comorbidity and its potential impact on treatment outcomes. Additionally, as suggested by Grant (2016), given that differences in outcomes between different treatments are often very small, larger studies are needed in order to effectively evaluate these differences. There is also a paucity of head-to-head trials of the different pharmacological agents or studies designed to address dose response and duration of treatment needed.

Another limitation is the heterogeneous nature of the PG population. Several models have been proposed in an attempt to explain this significant heterogeneity, including those proposed by Blaczczynski and Nower (2002) and Dannon et al. (2006). These models allow at least a conceptual framework in which to consider effective treatment recommendations. It is hoped that further research analysing the effectiveness of different pharmacologic agents in these proposed subgroups will be available in the future.

Without clear treatment guidelines for pharmacological interventions, therapies should perhaps be focused on suggested clinical dimensions (i.e. impulsivity, compulsivity, anhedonia) and/or on the comorbid psychiatric disorders that are frequently present. For example, it has been suggested that if the patient describes significant urges or cravings to gamble or has a co-occurring substance use disorder, an opioid antagonist should be considered (Grant and Kim 2006; Iancu et al. 2008). Similarly, if the person has co-occurring mood or anxiety symptoms or is displaying symptoms consistent with the 'obsessive-compulsive' subtype (Dannon et al. 2006), then an SSRI would be reasonable to consider. A mood stabiliser may be considered if the person gambles when hypo/manic symptoms are present or if there are features of the 'impulsive' subtype (Dannon et al. 2006; Iancu et al. 2008). Guidance regarding the use of glutamatergic agents is less clear, and these agents tend to be used less frequently in the clinical setting.

Importantly, to date, no existing treatment, either pharmacological or psycho-behavioural, is completely effective on its own. Combining both therapeutic modalities, as recommended in anxiety and mood disorders (Katzman et al. 2014; Malhi et al. 2015), is likely to yield better results and has been demonstrated in some studies (de Brito et al. 2017; Grant et al. 2014).

Case Study

David was a 37-year-old single man who lives in a rental property and worked casually as a barista. He presented to the clinic with a several-month history of pervasively low mood, increased irritability, sleep disturbance (with early morning waking) and weight loss. He also related decreased motivation to exercise or socialise, an inability to enjoy previous interests and hobbies and ruminative thoughts about 'how pointless my life has become'. Associated with these symptoms, David also described an increased intake of alcohol and had been drinking on an almost daily basis for the past few weeks. Since his late teens, David had always 'enjoyed putting a few bucks through the pokies'; however, over the past 6 weeks, he had been spending the most part of each day at the casino and had also commenced online gaming. David related a sense of 'escape' when he was gambling and found the monotonous action soothing. On prompting, David stated that he had accrued significant debts on several credit cards and owed money to several family members and close friends.

David was formulated as having a major depressive episode with melancholic features, likely triggered by the breakdown in a long-term relationship and perpetuated by his social isolation, financial stress and perceived loss of agency in regard to his gambling and alcohol use. Longitudinal assessment indicated that the increase in alcohol use and gambling seemed to be somewhat driven by his low mood and depressive symptoms.

David had a strong preference to trial non-pharmacological strategies, and so he proceeded to have a trial of CBT for approximately 4 weeks. Unfortunately, David missed several sessions and found it quite difficult to concentrate on the material discussed. He also lacked motivation to complete homework tasks. However, the sessions did seem helpful in assisting David to minimise his alcohol use, which in turn did decrease his losses from gambling. Although reduced, the PG retained its salience in David's life.

After he lost his job due to poor attendance, David was motivated to trial medication for his depressive symptoms. Following careful discussion around common side effects (nausea, headache, sexual dysfunction, possible sleep disturbance), David agreed to commencing sertraline. This was commenced at 25 mg for several days and then increased to 50 mg. David was seen regularly and the dose was titrated up to 100 mg. After 4 weeks of treatment, David felt his sleep was improved and was more motivated to seek further employment. He was able to abstain from alcohol. David also expressed interest in re-engaging with a psychologist for further CBT, and with the improvement in his depressive symptoms, he was now more able to concentrate and engage in the therapy.

References

Altshuler, H. L., Phillips, P. E., & Feinhandler, D. A. (1980). Alteration of ethanol self-administration by naltrexone. *Life Sciences, 26*(9), 679–688.

Association, A. P. (2013). *Diagnostic and statistical manual of mental disorders (DSM 5)*. Washington, DC: American Psychiatric Pub.

Australian Medicines Handbook. (2017). Retrieved from https://amhonline.amh.net.au/

Bartley, C. A., & Bloch, M. H. (2013). Meta-analysis: Pharmacological treatment of pathological gambling. *Expert Review of Neurotherapeutics, 13*(8), 887–894. doi:10.1586/14737175.2013.814938.

Benjamin, D., Grant, E. R., & Pohorecky, L. A. (1993). Naltrexone reverses ethanol-induced dopamine release in the nucleus accumbens in awake, freely moving rats. *Brain Research, 621*(1), 137–140.

Berlin, H. A., Braun, A., Simeon, D., Koran, L. M., Potenza, M. N., McElroy, S. L., Fong, T., Pallanti, S., & Hollander, E. (2013). A double-blind, placebo-controlled trial of topiramate for pathological gambling. *The World Journal of Biological Psychiatry, 14*(2), 121–128. doi:10.3109/15622975.2011.560964.

Black, D. W., Shaw, M., Forbush, K. T., & Allen, J. (2007). An open-label trial of escitalopram in the treatment of pathological gambling. *Clinical Neuropharmacology, 30*(4), 206–212. doi:10.1097/wnf.0b013e31803d357f.

Blanco, C., Petkova, E., Ibanez, A., & Saiz-Ruiz, J. (2002). A pilot placebo-controlled study of fluvoxamine for pathological gambling. *Annals of Clinical Psychiatry, 14*(1), 9–15.

Blaszczynski, A., & Nower, L. (2002). A pathways model of problem and pathological gambling. *Addiction, 97*(5), 487–499.

Claudino, A. M., de Oliveira, I. R., Appolinario, J. C., Cordas, T. A., Duchesne, M., Sichieri, R., & Bacaltchuk, J. (2007). Double-blind, randomized, placebo-controlled trial of topiramate plus cognitive-behavior therapy in binge-eating disorder. *The Journal of Clinical Psychiatry, 68*(9), 1324–1332.

Cowlishaw, S., Merkouris, S., Chapman, A., & Radermacher, H. (2014). Pathological and problem gambling in substance use treatment: A systematic review and meta-analysis. *Journal of Substance Abuse Treatment, 46*(2), 98–105. doi:10.1016/j.jsat.2013.08.019.

Cowlishaw, S., Merkouris, S., Dowling, N., Anderson, C., Jackson, A., & Thomas, S. (2012). Psychological therapies for pathological and problem gambling. *Cochrane Database of Systematic Reviews, 11*, CD008937. doi:10.1002/14651858.CD008937.pub2.

Dannon, P. N., Lowengrub, K., Gonopolski, Y., Musin, E., & Kotler, M. (2006). Pathological gambling: A review of phenomenological models and treatment modalities for an underrecognized psychiatric disorder. *Primary Care Companion Journal of Clinical Psychiatry, 8*(6), 334–339.

de Brito, A. M., de Almeida Pinto, M. G., Bronstein, G., Carneiro, E., Faertes, D., Fukugawa, V., Duque, A., Vasconcellos, F., & Tavares, H. (2017). Topiramate combined with cognitive restructuring for the treatment of gambling disorder: A two-center, randomized, double-blind clinical trial. *Journal of Gambling Studies, 33*(1), 249–263. doi:10.1007/s10899-016-9620-z.

Di Nicola, M., De Risio, L., Pettorruso, M., Caselli, G., De Crescenzo, F., Swierkosz-Lenart, K., Martinotti G, Camardese G, Di Giannantonio M., & Janiri, L. (2014). Bipolar disorder and gambling disorder comorbidity: Current evidence and implications for pharmacological treatment. Journal of Affective Disorders, 167, 285–298. 10.1016/j.jad.2014.06.023.

Dowling, N. A., Merkouris, S. S., & Lorains, F. K. (2016). Interventions for comorbid problem gambling and psychiatric disorders: Advancing a developing field of research. *Addictive Behaviors, 58*, 21–30. doi:10.1016/j.addbeh.2016.02.012.

Grant, J. E., & Chamberlain, S. R. (2016). Pharmacotherapy for behavioral addictions. *Current Behavioral Neuroscience Reports, 3*, 67–72.

Grant, J. E., & Kim, S. W. (2006). Medication management of pathological gambling. *Minnesota Medicine, 89*(9), 44–48.

Grant, J. E., Chamberlain, S. R., Odlaug, B. L., Potenza, M. N., & Kim, S. W. (2010). Memantine shows promise in reducing gambling severity and cognitive inflexibility in pathological gambling: A pilot study. *Psychopharmacology, 212*(4), 603–612. doi:10.1007/s00213-010-1994-5.

Grant, J. E., Kim, S. W., Hollander, E., & Potenza, M. N. (2008). Predicting response to opiate antagonists and placebo in the treatment of pathological gambling. *Psychopharmacology, 200*(4), 521–527. doi:10.1007/s00213-008-1235-3.

Grant, J. E., Kim, S. W., & Odlaug, B. L. (2007). N-acetyl cysteine, a glutamate-modulating agent, in the treatment of pathological gambling: A pilot study. *Biological Psychiatry, 62*(6), 652–657. doi:10.1016/j.biopsych.2006.11.021.

Grant, J. E., Kim, S. W., Potenza, M. N., Blanco, C., Ibanez, A., Stevens, L., Hektner, J. M., & Zaninelli, R. (2003). Paroxetine treatment of pathological gambling: A multi-centre randomized controlled trial. *International Clinical Psychopharmacology, 18*(4), 243–249. doi:10.1097/01.yic.0000073881.93678.21.

Grant, J. E., Odlaug, B. L., & Chamberlain, S. R. (2016). Neural and psychological underpinnings of gambling disorder: A review. *Progress in Neuro-Psychopharmacology & Biological Psychiatry, 65*, 188–193. doi:10.1016/j.pnpbp.2015.10.007.

Grant, J. E., Odlaug, B. L., Chamberlain, S. R., Potenza, M. N., Schreiber, L. R., Donahue, C. B., & Kim, S. W. (2014). A randomized, placebo-controlled trial of N-acetylcysteine plus imaginal desensitization for nicotine-dependent pathological gamblers. *The Journal of Clinical Psychiatry, 75*(1), 39–45. doi:10.4088/JCP.13m08411.

Grant, J. E., & Potenza, M. N. (2006). Escitalopram treatment of pathological gambling with co-occurring anxiety: An open-label pilot study with double-blind discontinuation. *International Clinical Psychopharmacology, 21*(4), 203–209.

Hemby, S. E., Tang, W., Muly, E. C., Kuhar, M. J., Howell, L., & Mash, D. C. (2005). Cocaine-induced alterations in nucleus accumbens ionotropic glutamate receptor subunits in human and non-human primates. *Journal of Neurochemistry, 95*(6), 1785–1793. doi:10.1111/j.1471-4159.2005.03517.x.

Hollander, E., Buchsbaum, M. S., Haznedar, M. M., Berenguer, J., Berlin, H. A., Chaplin, W., et al. (2008). FDG-PET study in pathological gamblers. 1. Lithium increases orbitofrontal, dorsolateral and cingulate metabolism. *Neuropsychobiology, 58*(1), 37–47. doi:10.1159/000154478.

Hollander, E., DeCaria, C. M., Finkell, J. N., Begaz, T., Wong, C. M., & Cartwright, C. (2000). A randomized double-blind fluvoxamine/placebo crossover trial in pathologic gambling. *Biological Psychiatry, 47*(9), 813–817.

Hollander, E., Pallanti, S., Allen, A., Sood, E., & Baldini Rossi, N. (2005). Does sustained-release lithium reduce impulsive gambling and affective instability versus placebo in pathological gamblers with bipolar spectrum disorders? *The American Journal of Psychiatry, 162*(1), 137–145. doi:10.1176/appi.ajp.162.1.137.

Iancu, I., Lowengrub, K., Dembinsky, Y., Kotler, M., & Dannon, P. N. (2008). Pathological gambling: An update on neuropathophysiology and pharmacotherapy. *CNS Drugs, 22*(2), 123–138.

Johnson, B. A., Rosenthal, N., Capece, J. A., Wiegand, F., Mao, L., Beyers, K., McKay, A., Ait-Daoud, N., Anton, R. F., Ciraulo, D. A., Kranzler, H. R., Mann, K., O'Malley, S. S., Swift, R. M., & Topiramate for Alcoholism Study, G. (2007). Topiramate for treating alcohol dependence: A randomized controlled trial. *JAMA, 298*(14), 1641–1651. doi:10.1001/jama.298.14.1641.

Kalivas, P. W. (2009). The glutamate homeostasis hypothesis of addiction. *Nature Reviews. Neuroscience, 10*(8), 561–572. doi:10.1038/nrn2515.

Kalivas, P. W., & Volkow, N. D. (2011). New medications for drug addiction hiding in glutamatergic neuroplasticity. *Molecular Psychiatry, 16*(10), 974–986. doi:10.1038/mp.2011.46.

Katzman, M. A., Bleau, P., Blier, P., Chokka, P., Kjernisted, K., Van Ameringen, M., Canadian Anxiety Guidelines Initiative Group on behalf of the Anxiety Disorders Association of Canada/Association Canadienne des troubles anxieux and McGill University, Antony, M. M., Bouchard, S., Brunet, A., Flament, M., Grigoriadis, S., Mendlowitz, S., O'Connor, K., Rabheru, K., Richter, P. M., Robichaud, M., & Walker, J. R. (2014). Canadian clinical practice guidelines for the management of anxiety, posttraumatic stress and obsessive-compulsive disorders. *BMC Psychiatry, 14*(Suppl 1), S1. doi:10.1186/1471-244X-14-S1-S1.

Kim, S. W. (1998). Opioid antagonists in the treatment of impulse-control disorders. *The Journal of Clinical Psychiatry, 59*(4), 159–164.

Kim, S. W., Grant, J. E., Adson, D. E., Shin, Y. C., & Zaninelli, R. (2002). A double-blind placebo-controlled study of the efficacy and safety of paroxetine in the treatment of pathological gambling. *The Journal of Clinical Psychiatry, 63*(6), 501–507.

Labuzek, K., Beil, S., Beil-Gawelczyk, J., Gabryel, B., Franik, G., & Okopien, B. (2014). The latest achievements in the pharmacotherapy of gambling disorder. *Pharmacological Reports, 66*(5), 811–820. doi:10.1016/j.pharep.2014.05.003.

Malhi, G. S., Bassett, D., Boyce, P., Bryant, R., Fitzgerald, P. B., Fritz, K., Hopwood, M., Lyndon, B., Mulder, R., Murray, G., Porter, R., & Singh, A. B. (2015). Royal Australian and New Zealand College of Psychiatrists clinical practice guidelines for mood disorders. *The Australian and New Zealand Journal of Psychiatry, 49*(12), 1087–1206. doi:10.1177/0004867415617657.

Pallanti, S., Quercioli, L., Sood, E., & Hollander, E. (2002). Lithium and valproate treatment of pathological gambling: A randomized single-blind study. *The Journal of Clinical Psychiatry, 63*(7), 559–564.

Petry, N. M., Ammerman, Y., Bohl, J., Doersch, A., Gay, H., Kadden, R., Molina, C., & Steinberg, K. (2006). Cognitive-behavioral therapy for pathological gamblers. *Journal of Consulting and Clinical Psychology, 74*(3), 555–567. doi:10.1037/0022-006X.74.3.555.

Petry, N. M., Blanco, C., Auriacombe, M., Borges, G., Bucholz, K., Crowley, T. J., Grant, B. F., Hasin, D. S., & O'Brien, C. (2014). An overview of and rationale for changes proposed for pathological gambling in DSM-5. *Journal of Gambling Studies, 30*(2), 493–502. doi:10.1007/s10899-013-9370-0.

Piquet-Pessoa, M., & Fontenelle, L. F. (2016). Opioid antagonists in broadly defined behavioral addictions: A narrative review. *Expert Opinion on Pharmacotherapy, 17*(6), 835–844. doi:10.1517/14656566.2016.1145660.

Saiz-Ruiz, J., Blanco, C., Ibanez, A., Masramon, X., Gomez, M. M., Madrigal, M., & Diez, T. (2005). Sertraline treatment of pathological gambling: A pilot study. *The Journal of Clinical Psychiatry, 66*(1), 28–33.

Thomas, A., Bonanni, L., Gambi, F., Di Iorio, A., & Onofrj, M. (2010). Pathological gambling in Parkinson disease is reduced by amantadine. *Annals of Neurology, 68*(3), 400–404. doi:10.1002/ana.22029.

van den Brink, W. (2012). Evidence-based pharmacological treatment of substance use disorders and pathological gambling. *Current Drug Abuse Reviews, 5*(1), 3–31.

van Wageningen, H., Jorgensen, H. A., Specht, K., & Hugdahl, K. (2010). A 1H-MR spectroscopy study of changes in glutamate and glutamine (Glx) concentrations in frontal spectra after administration of memantine. *Cerebral Cortex, 20*(4), 798–803. doi:10.1093/cercor/bhp145.

Vornik, L. A., & Brown, E. S. (2006). Management of comorbid bipolar disorder and substance abuse. *The Journal of Clinical Psychiatry, 67*(Suppl 7), 24–30.

Chapter 10
Relapse Prevention in Problem Gambling

Katy O'Neill

A Long and Winding Road

The path out of problem gambling is a complex, iterative journey with many twists and turns. So much so that when a sample of recovered problem gamblers were asked if they had any advice to help an active problem gambler, half of them indicated that, "there was nothing that could be done to aid in this process" (Toneatto et al. 2008, page 116).

The gambling treatment literature is replete with high rates of treatment dropouts and relapse (Aragay et al. 2015; Petry 2005). The success rates of treated gamblers can be compared to the success rates of problem gamblers who recover without treatment. Slutske (2006) looked at prevalence rates for lifetime and past year pathological gambling in two US nationwide surveys. She found that between 36% and 39% of those who had at one time in their life met the criteria for a diagnosis of pathological gambling no longer met those criteria in the past year. One third of recoveries from problem gambling could be classified as natural recovery (i.e. without treatment), half of which were stable recoveries of 5 years or more. Stable recovery, however, is by no means a typical pathway towards recovery (Nixon and Solowoniuk 2006; Reith and Dobbie 2013; Blaszczynski et al. 1991).

Complex trajectories speak to relapse rates and the difficulty of change, but they also reveal individuals successfully learning from experience (Oakes et al. 2012a, b, Vasiliadis and Thomas 2016). This is true for both those who recover unaided and with the assistance of treatment. People learn from treatment episodes, even if they do not recover on their first attempt. Hodgins and El-Guebaly (2004) reported that recovered gamblers who had sought treatment in the past used a greater number of

K. O'Neill (✉)
St Vincent's Hospital Gambling Treatment Program, St Vincent's Hospital,
390 Victoria St, Darlinghurst, Sydney, NSW 2010, Australia
e-mail: ko@kogo.net.au

C. McIntosh, K. O'Neill, *Evidence-Based Treatments for Problem Gambling*,
SpringerBriefs in Psychology, DOI 10.1007/978-3-319-62485-3_10

change strategies in their attempts to quit. Jackson et al. (2008) suggested that representing for a second or later episode of treatment has traditionally been viewed as a sign of failure. Jackson et al. found, however, that representers were likely to achieve positive outcomes from treatment. They propose that treatment episodes can be understood as interactive, incremental and cumulative.

Tucker and King (1999) suggest that given the ubiquity of unsuccessful quit attempts, many addicts encounter circumstances that motivate change, but fewer encounter circumstances that maintain it. Specifically, Tucker and colleagues noted that negative events motivate attempts to control or cease substance abuse, while positive events help maintain the new lifestyle. Hodgins and colleagues (1999, 2000) reported a similar pattern in recovered gamblers.

The ideas that recovery is a complex journey, that lapses are highly probable and that one can learn to respond differently to lapses and that changes in behaviour contribute to changes in life events which in turn help in recovery are all very much part of the widely influential relapse prevention model proposed by Marlatt and Gordon (1985).

Marlatt and Gordon's Relapse Prevention Model

When Marlatt and Gordon published *Relapse Prevention: Maintenance Strategies in the Treatment of Addictive Behaviours* in 1985, viewing relapse as a process rather than an outcome was a new approach. Indeed, research into instances of natural recovery or trajectories of recovery as described above was novel. Key to their approach was identifying triggers and early warning signs, using coping skills in high-risk situations, differentiating between a lapse and a full-blown relapse and avoiding throwing in the towel and giving up altogether following a lapse – the abstinence violation effect (AVE). Clinical trials of relapse prevention (RP) for a range of substance use disorders were successful (Carroll 1996).

RP for Problem Gambling

Writing in 2005, Shaffer and LaPlante noted that there had been a paucity of research addressing the effectiveness of RP in the gambling field. Nonetheless, in a review of the problem gambling treatment literature, Korn and Shaffer noted that the strength of the evidence for RP was moderate (Korn and Shaffer 2004). RP modules have justifiably been routinely included in treatment protocols (Milton 2001; Ladouceur et al. 2002; Ladouceur and Lachance 2007; Petry 2005; Raylu and Oei 2010).

A randomised trial of RP for problem gamblers was conducted by Echeburua, Fernandez-Montalvo and Baez in 2000. This was the first study of RP as an isolated component of therapy rather than as one component embedded in a treatment package.

After successful treatment, gamblers were randomly assigned to individual or group RP aftercare or a control group (assessment only). The individual and group RP conditions were equivalent and achieved significantly higher success rates (82.6% and 78.3% recovered, respectively) than the control group (55% recovered.) The RP package was based on Marlatt and Gordon's RP model.

Relapse in PG

Ledgerwood and Petry in 2006 lamented that there were few empirical studies of relapse in pathological gambling. This remains the case (Aragay et al. 2015). It is yet not clear, for example, how closely the high-risk situations for alcohol and substance use described in Marlatt and Gordon's original model apply to the high-risk situations commonly identified in problem gambling. While many relapse triggers overlap (e.g. escaping negative emotions), there is one particular cognitive difference between relapse to problem gambling and relapse to substance use. One last drink can never make good all the past hurts. But in gambling, the fantasy of quitting after one last big win, big enough to reverse the damage done to loved ones, before finally quitting persists. This relapse-inducing fallacy even has its own name – the gambler's conceit.

Hodgins and el-Guebaly (2004) provided the first description of relapse precipitants for gambling problems obtained from a naturalistic sample followed prospectively. They found that the categorization of relapse precipitants in a sample of problem gamblers were very different to Marlatt's taxonomy. In Marlatt's categorization, intrapersonal and interpersonal negative emotional states predominate, whereas for problem gamblers, cognitive and financial aspects (such as optimism about winning or a need to make money) were more likely to precede lapses. Similarly, Echeburua and Fernandez-Montalvo (2005) found that the main trigger of relapse was inadequate money management.

Toneatto (2005) noted that "unlike the chemical addictions, where cessation can reasonably be expected to lead to improvement in most areas of functioning, the cessation of gambling may be only the beginning of the process of coping with serious or intractable financial problems which may be shared with significant others and endure for many years". He notes, "the financial repercussions may be beyond what psychological treatments can reasonably impact upon, yet such long-term debt may contribute to relapse and contribute to ambivalence" (page 79).

Pathological gamblers are more likely to rehearse positive rather than negative outcomes of gambling scenarios as indicated by responses on a modified Stroop task (Atkins and Sharpe, cited in Sharpe 2002). Furthermore, research has shown that problem gamblers show heightened autonomic arousal in the presence of gambling cues (Ledgerwood and Petry 2006). Urges are the combination of such physiological states and the gambling related cognitions that are elicited. Sharpe (2002) describes the interplay between triggers, arousal and expectancies that make up a gambling urge: "Gambling-related problems can make the weighted importance of winning seem so enormous that losing further seems inconsequential, contributing to the cognitive biases that perpetuate gambling" (Sharpe 2002, page 20).

The identification of high-risk situations and the acknowledgement that one's thinking can be altered in these situations are a critical component of Ladouceur and colleagues' cognitive behavioural therapy for problem gambling (Ladouceur et al. 2002). Describing the behavioural chain of excessive gambling, Ladouceur and colleagues explain to clients "a situation or event marks the first step in the chain. The urge to gamble always surfaces within a particular context… this context, which is usually a risky situation, generates risky thoughts that activate the urge to gamble" Ladouceur et al. 2002, page 31.

Predicting Relapse

Research attempts to predict the likelihood of relapse to problem gambling using personality measures have generally been inconsistent (Blasszczynski et al. 1991; Dowling et al. 2009) with the possible exception of impulsivity (Sharpe 2002; Ledgerwood and Petry 2006). Echeburua and Ferndandez-Montalvo (2005) concluded that situational elements rather than personality dimensions were more important in predicting relapse and that this should generate therapeutic optimism. Focusing on situations, the RP model did provide a helpful heuristic and treatment framework. Nonetheless, criticisms of Marlatt's earlier classifications of relapse triggers included a lack of emphasis on urges as well as not allowing adequately for idiosyncrasies in an interactive, fluctuating process (Marlatt and Witkiewitz 2005).

Taking on board such criticisms, the previously linear RP model was reconceptualised into a multidimensional and dynamic model which includes feedback loops between tonic processes, phasic responses, distal risks and contextual factors (Witkiewitz and Marlatt 2004). This model is compatible with mathematical models that describe the behaviour of complex systems such as catastrophe and chaos theories. Witkiewitz et al. (2007) successfully applied one such "dynamical systems" mathematical model to data sets from Project MATCH (a multisite alcohol treatment study). West (2006) also suggested that chaos theory is useful, at least as a metaphor for the transition from an addicted state to a not-addicted state.

McCown and Chamberlain (2000) applied chaos theory specifically to relapse in gambling addiction. They noted that "one of many implications of chaos theory is the apparent paradox of phenomena that are simultaneously completely causally determined but essentially still mostly entirely unpredictable" (page 184). "Chaotic phenomena although unpredictable are not random" (page 188). Examples might be the pattern of smoke rising or the flow of eddies in a stream of water as well as lapses and recovery from problem gambling. They note that, "at specific and identifiable critical periods in the process of recovery, problem gamblers may be extraordinarily influenced by very small events, which may have extreme and unpredictable implications for future functioning… sensitivity to initial conditions explains both relapse and the desire to recover" (page 193).

Overall, the implication is that it is difficult to predict relapse. Clinically, however, individuals can usefully learn from their lapses or relapses. To paraphrase the Danish philosopher Kierkegaard – life can only be understood backwards, but it must be lived forwards. Problem gambling clients can identify their own distal factors or early warning signs, their own proximal factors or high-risk situations and their own internal and external triggers. A recent extension of relapse prevention programme does this by incorporating mindfulness (Bowen et al. 2011)

Mindfulness-Based Relapse Prevention

Mindfulness meditation has been incorporated into treatment protocols and successfully applied to pain management (mindfulness-based stress reduction (MBSR)) and to depression (mindfulness-based cognitive therapy (MBCT)). Based on the success of these therapies, Witkiewitz, Marlatt and colleagues proposed a protocol which formally integrates mindfulness and relapse prevention (Witkiewitz et al. 2005).

How does mindfulness-based relapse prevention (MBRP) differ from standard RP? Bowen et al. (2014) note that despite the supporting evidence from clinical trials, RP has some potential shortcomings. Although urge surfing has always been a component of RP, there has been an emphasis on avoidance of high-risk situations or the use of alternative coping behaviours to attempt to control the causes of negative affect. MBRP, however, extended the mindfulness approach to the full range of life experiences beyond just a strategy for dealing with urges.

MBRP in the format of an 8-week aftercare programme was evaluated in a pilot study where it was compared to treatment as usual (TAU) (8 weeks of standard aftercare delivered in a 12-step group format) (Bowen et al. 2009). In this study, MBRP was shown to be as effective at 4-month follow-up as TAU. It was also found to be acceptable to clients and feasible in that most clients did some mindfulness meditation practice at home. More recently, Bowen et al. (2014) compared MBRP with standard RP and with TAU (12-step oriented programme) at 3-, 6- and 12-month follow-up. At 3 months, there was no difference between the groups. At 6 months, both the RP groups showed significantly less relapse than the TAU group. By 12 months, the MBRP group had better outcomes than the standard RP group and the TAU group. The authors suggest that the more enduring effect of MBRP is explained by the participants' improved ability to recognise and tolerate discomfort associated with craving or negative affect due to continued practice of the MBRP skills over time. Although they do not indicate what skills, they reported that over 88% of the participants in the MBRP group said they were using skills from the programme at least once a week.

A clinician's guide to the MBRP programme is available (Bowen et al. 2011). This describes the eight-session programme in detail. Each session consists of psychoeducation with handouts, a mindfulness meditation practice, group discussion and home practice. Throughout the programme, mindfulness practices are applied to the range of experiences associated with relapse – feelings, thoughts, reactions and triggers.

MBRP has not yet been evaluated for problem gamblers. However, both standard RP and mindfulness have been found to be effective in the treatment of problem gamblers (Echeburura et al. 2000; Echeburua and Fernandez-Montalvo 2005; McIntosh et al. 2016. See the Metacognitive and Mindfulness chapter in this book).

Life Is More than Not Gambling

As noted above, people recovering from gambling may experience more difficulties than those recovering from other substances in restoring relationships or taking up new passions for several reasons. McCown and Chamberlain (2000) observe that whereas people in early recovery from substance abuse often feel somewhat better quite quickly because they begin to reclaim some of their health, it may take months for problem gamblers to experience a sense of hopefulness in the face of overwhelming financial and relationship problems (page 130). Trust may take longer to re-establish for gamblers than for other substances. The families of those recovering from substance use can more easily see signs of relapse, but because relapse to gambling is harder to detect immediately, it may take years before the gambler earns back the trust of family members or business partners. Furthermore, the financial situation left by the gambling may take many years to repair, and this may severely limit new options and impact on the family (Toneatto 2005).

RP programmes emphasise the importance of lifestyle balance in long-term maintenance. In a proof of concept study, Jackson et al. (2013) noted that problem gamblers often engage in few social activities other than gambling. After treatment, they can be left with considerable unstructured time and inadequate social skills and feelings of emptiness and boredom. The (Re)Making Meaning Project was a 9-month programme focusing on normalising non-gambling leisure in which former problem gamblers sampled various activities such as barbeques, computer lessons and French Jive lessons with community volunteers. Despite dropouts, the results were promising enough to warrant further research.

People quit gambling for a reason. Quitting gambling may initially involve an avoidance goal (they might quit to avoid financial ruin and emotional pain). Continuing to refrain from gambling may involve an approach goal (reconnecting relationships, doing long-needed repairs around the home, taking a family holiday, travelling, studying or resuming an abandoned passion such as music or sport). It is not enough just to stop gambling. One also stops gambling when one dies. Recovering from problem gambling is done in the service of life.

References

Aragay, N., Jimenez-Murcia, S., Granero, R., Fernandez-Aranda, F., Ramos-Grille, I., Cardona, S., Garrido, G., Islam, M. A., Menchon, J. M., & Valles, V. (2015). Pathological gambling: Understanding relapses and dropouts. *Comprehensive Psychiatry, 57*, 58–64. doi:10.1016/j.comppsych.2014.10.009.

Blaszczynski, A., McConaghy, N., & Frankova, A. (1991). A comparison of relapsed and non-relapsed abstinent pathological gamblers following behavioural treatment. *British Journal of Addiction, 86*, 1485–1489.

Bowen, S., Chawla, N., Collins, S. E., Witkiewitz, K., Hsu, S., Grow, J., Clifasefi, S., Garner, M., Douglass, A., Larimer, M. E., & Marlatt, A. (2009). Mindfulness-based relapse prevention for substance use disorders: A pilot efficacy trial. *Substance Abuse, 30*, 295–305. doi:10.1080/08897070903250084.

Bowen, S., Chawla, N., & Marlatt, G. A. (2011). *Mindfulness-based relapse prevention for addictive behaviors: A clinician's guide*. New York: The Guilford Press.

Bowen, S., Witkiewitz, K., Clifasefi, S. L., Grow, J., Chawla, N., Hsu, S. H., Carroll, H. A., Harrop, E., Collins, S. E., Lustyk, K., & Larimer, M. E. (2014). Relative efficacy of mindfulness-based relapse prevention, standard relapse prevention, and treatment as usual for substance use disorders: A randomized clinical trial. *JAMA Psychiatry, 71*(5), 547–556. doi:10.1001/jamapsychiatry.2013.4546.

Carroll, K. M. (1996). Relapse prevention as a psychosocial treatment: A review of controlled clinical trials. *Experimental and Clinical Psychopharmacology, 4*(1), 46–54.

Dowling, N., Smith, D., & Thomas, T. (2009). A comparison of individual and group cognitive-behavioural treatment for female pathological gambling. *Behaviour Research and Therapy, 45*, 2192–2202.

Echeburua, E., & Fernandez-Montalvo, J. (2005). Psychological treatment of slot-machine pathological gambling: New perspectives. *Journal of Gambling Studies, 21*(1), 21–26. doi:10.1007/s10899-004-1918-6.

Echeburua, E., Fernandez-Montalvo, J., & Baez, C. (2000). Relapse prevention in the treatment of slot-machine pathological gambling: Long-term outcome. *Behavior Therapy, 31*, 351–364.

Hodgins, D. C., & el-Guebaly, N. (2000). Natural and treatment-assisted recovery from gambling problems: A comparison of resolved and active gamblers. *Addiction, 95*(5), 777–789.

Hodgins, D. C., & el-Guebaly, N. (2004). Retrospective and prospective reports of precipitants to relapse in pathological gambling. *Journal of Consulting and Clinical Psychology, 72*(1), 72–80. doi:10.1037/0022-006X.72.1.72.

Hodgins, D. C., Wynne, H., & Makarchuck, K. (1999). Pathways to recovery from gambling problems: Follow-up from a general population survey. *Journal of Gambling Studies, 15*(2), 93–104.

Jackson, A. C., Dowling, N., Thomas, S. A., & Holt, T. A. (2008). Treatment careers in problem gambling: Factors associated with first treatment and treatment re-entry. *Addiction Research and Theory, 16*(6), 618–632. doi:10.1080/16066350802008793.

Jackson, A. C., Francis, K. L., Byrne, G., & Christensen, D. R. (2013). Leisure substitution and problem gambling: Report of a proof of concept group intervention. *International Journal of Mental Health and Addiction, 11*, 64–74. doi:10.1007/s11469-012-9399-9.

Korn, D. A., & Shaffer, H. J. (2004). *Practice guidelines for treating gambling-related problems*. Toronto: Massachusetts Council on Compulsive Gambling.

Ladouceur, R., & Lachance, S. (2007). *Overcoming pathological gambling. Therapist guide*. Oxford: Oxford University Press.

Ladouceur, R., Sylvain, C., Boutin, C., & Doucet, C. (2002). *Understanding and treating the pathological gambler*. Chichester: John Wiley and Sons.

Ledgerwood, D. M., & Petry, N. M. (2006). What do we know about relapse in pathological gambling? *Clinical Psychology Review, 26*, 216–228. doi:10.1016/j.cpr.2005.11.008.

Marlatt, G.A., & Gordon, J. (1985). *Relapse prevention: Maintenance strategies in the treatment of addictive behaviours*. New York: The Guilford Press.

Marlatt, G. A., & Witkiewitz, K. (2005). Relapse prevention for alcohol and drug problems. In G. A. Marlatt & D. M. Donovan (Eds.), *Relapse prevention: Maintenance strategies in the treatment of addictive behaviors* (2nd ed.). New York: Guilford Press.

McCown, W. G., & Chamberlain, L. L. (2000). *Best possible odds: Contemporary treatment strategies for gambling disorders*. New York: John Wiley & Sons.

McIntosh, C. C., Crino, R. D., & O'Neill, K. (2016). Treating problem gambling samples with cognitive behavioural therapy and mindfulness-based interventions. *A clinical trial. Journal of Gambling Studies, 32*, 1305–1325. doi:10.1007/s10899-016-9602-1.

Milton, S. (2001). *Stop gambling: A self-help manual for giving up gambling*. Sydney: Pan Macmillan.

Nixon, G., & Solowoniuk, J. (2006). An insider's look into the process of recovering from pathological gambling disorder: An existential phenomenological inquiry. *International Journal of Mental Health and Addiction, 4*, 119–132. doi:10.1007/s11469-006-9012-1.

Oakes, J., Pols, R., Battersby, M., Lawn, S., Pulvirenti, M., & Smith, D. (2012a). A focus group study of predictors of relapse in electronic gaming machine problem gambling, part 1: Factors that 'push' towards relapse. *Journal of Gambling Studies, 28*, 451–464. doi:10.1007/s10899-011-9264-y.

Oakes, J., Pols, R., Battersby, M., Lawn, S., Pulvirenti, M., & Smith, D. (2012b). A focus group study of predictors of relapse in electronic gaming machine problem gambling, part 2: Factors that 'pull' the gambler away from relapse. *Journal of Gambling Studies, 28*, 465–479. doi:10.1007/s10899-011-9267-8.

Petry, N. M. (2005). *Pathological gambling: Etiology, comorbidity, and treatment*. Washington: American Psychological Association.

Raylu, N., & Oei, T. P. (2010). *A cognitive behavioural therapy programme for problem gambling: Therapist manual*. London: Routledge.

Reith, G., & Dobbie, F. (2013). Gambling careers: A longitudinal, qualitative study of gambling behaviour. *Addiction Research and Theory, 21*(5), 376–390. doi:10.3109/16066359.2012.731116.

Shaffer, H. J., & LaPlante, D. A. (2005). Treatment of gambling disorders. In G. A. Marlatt & D. M. Donovan (Eds.), *Relapse prevention: Maintenance strategies in the treatment of addictive behaviors* (2nd ed.). New York: Guilford Press.

Sharpe, L. (2002). A reformulated cognitive-behavioral model of problem gambling: A biopsychosocial perspective. *Clinical Psychology Review, 22*, 1–25.

Slutse, W. S. (2006). Natural recovery and treatment-seeking in pathological gambling: Results of two U.S. national surveys. *American Journal of Psychiatry, 163*(2), 297–302.

Toneatto, T. (2005). A perspective on problem gambling treatment: Issues and challenges. *Journal of Gambling Studies, 21*(1), 75–80. doi:10.10007/s10899-004-1925-7.

Toneatto, T., Cunningham, J., Hodgins, D., Adams, M., Turner, N., & Koski-jannes, A. (2008). Recovery from problem gambling without formal treatment. *Addiction Research and Theory, 16*(2), 111–120. doi:10.1080/16066350801923638.

Tucker, J. A., & King, M. P. (1999). Resolving alcohol and drug problems: Influences on addictive behavior change and help-seeking processes. In J. A. Tucker, D. M. Donovan, & G. A. Marlatt (Eds.), *Changing addictive behavior*. New York: The Guilford Press.

Vasiliadis, S., & Thomas, A. (2016). *Journeys through gambling: Pathways to informal recovery*. Melbourne: Victorian Responsible Gambling Foundation.

West, R. (2006). *Theory of addiction*. Oxford: Blackwell Publishing.

Witkiewitz, K., & Marlatt, G. A. (2004). Relapse prevention for alcohol and drug problems: That was zen, this is tao. *American Psychologist, 59*(4), 224–235. doi:10.1037/0003-066X.59.4.224.

Witkiewitz, K., Marlatt, G. A., & Walker, D. (2005). Mindfulness-based relapse prevention for alcohol and substance use disorders. *Journal of Cognitive Psychotherapy: An international quarterly, 19*(3), 211–228.

Witkiewitz, K., van der Maas, H. L. J., Hufford, M. R., & Marlatt, G. A. (2007). Nonnormality and divergence in posttreatment alcohol use: Reexamining the project MATCH data 'another way'. *Journal of Abnormal Psychology, 116*(2), 378–394. doi:10.1037/0021-843X.116.2.378.

Druck:
Canon Deutschland Business Services GmbH
im Auftrag der KNV-Gruppe
Ferdinand-Jühlke-Str. 7
99095 Erfurt